When Helping Works

When Helping Works

Alleviating Fear and Pain in Global Missions

Michael Bamwesigye Badriaki

Foreword by Randy S. Woodley

WIPF & STOCK · Eugene, Oregon

WHEN HELPING WORKS
Alleviating Fear and Pain in Global Missions

Wipf & Stock
An Imprint of Wipf and Stock Publishers
199 W. 8th Ave., Suite 3
Eugene, OR 97401

www.wipfandstock.com

PAPERBACK ISBN: 978-1-5326-0893-3
HARDCOVER ISBN: 978-1-5326-0895-7
EBOOK ISBN: 978-1-5326-0894-0

Manufactured in the U.S.A.   APRIL 12, 2021

Contents

Foreword

MICHAEL BADRIAKI IS ABOUT to take you on an important dialogical journey simply for the cost of his book. With over twenty years of experience working in Africa, Asia, the UK, Haiti, and America, Michael Badriaki knows how to go deep into the areas vexing our own souls and consciences with a gentleness that perhaps only a person who has participated in both sides of Christian mission and international development work could accomplish.

This book will challenge the wrong stereotypes that we have created within our Christian mission systems. The idea behind the "stereotype" comes from the ancient Greek word *stereos*, which means "solid" or "firm." *Tupos*, means an "engraved mark." Together, they signify a "real mark" or "solid impression." Perhaps the Greeks did not invent the idea of stereotype, but from their earliest literature and art we know they developed well the ideas of the "savage" or "barbarian" and what I refer to in the missional world as "the cultural other." Over thousands of years, Western civilization has been upholding these myths throughout the historical realities of colonialism, slavery, racism, etc. The West has now come to realize they, indeed, are our myths. In *When Helping Works*, Michael helps us to understand where these negative stereotype threats in the church lay silent and unspoken and he assists the missional thinker in finding new paths forward.

You may notice the similarity of this title to another book of similar subject matter—this is not an accident but rather a constructive response and a better way to move forward in mission. As a sage way into the discussion, in the introduction and mainly in chapters one and two of the book, Michael provides some insights as a critique of the mind-set in Western evangelical literature on missions. Although not an entire review of their book, he argues for an alternative approach to Brian Fikkert and Steve Corbett's book *When Helping Hurts*.

This critique is necessary because of the wide-spread notoriety among churches that the book has gained and because of what it lacks. A notoriety, I might add, that is partially well-deserved, but still fails in the same manner as most Western writers do concerning missions. In Badriaki's view, the book misses the mark of majority world perspectives present in the global church and fails to take into account the need for the proper representation of those lives and cultures. Without recognizing it, many Western writers continue to promote paternalism and its effort to sentimentalize, essentialize, normalize, and glamorize the Western heroic missionary's privilege, creating again "the cultural other." Such shaping of Western evangelical's practices and understanding about doing missions in places like Africa and other parts of the world continues to encourage negative stereotype threat. What's more, the consequent outlook suffers from the invisibility of those who are not presented as problem solvers, but are rather portrayed as the problem.

In this book, Michael provides a positive and corrective perspective about the love ethic of helping neighbor, which he argues is in contrast to Fikkert and Corbett's mind-set, as it attempts to scapegoat and marginalize the art of helping, at the expense of redressing some of the core issues of identity he raises in the book.

For years, sincere, well-meaning, Western missional folks have been asking, "How do we do mission right?" If you are willing to look deep into the stereotype threats in our society and our own souls, Michael Badriaki will reveal in this book not only how to do mission right, but how to do mission well.

Dr. Randy S. Woodley, PhD
Author of *Shalom and the Community of Creation: An Indigenous Vision*
Distinguished professor of faith and culture
Director of Intercultural and Indigenous Studies
George Fox University

Acknowledgments

MANY PEOPLE HAVE BEEN very supportive along this journey. To my bride and best friend Kristen Ann Badriaki and our bright and beautiful daughter Teniel. Thank you for the love and encouragement you have extended to me from the start to the completion of this book. I dedicate this book to both of you. I am grateful to both my mother and father who love me and instilled in me the love for learning, community, and listening. Thanks to my parents-in-law for their support, my extend family, teachers, and friends as well. Thanks to Dr. Krish Kandiah, who published an interview in the magazine Christian Today in which we discussed some of the issues I further explain at length in this book. I am indebted to my friend Dr. Randy Woodley who agreed to write a foreword for the book. Dr. Woodley is a distinguished professor of faith and culture and director of Intercultural and Indigenous Studies at George Fox University. The Woodleys have extended a warm hand of fellowship to their home and Eloheh Farm. I am more than grateful that he is a caring and insightful teacher and I have the deepest appreciation for him!

I am grateful for my dear friends Brandi and Duane Butler, for their care and willingness to read through and edit this book. For further information, please visit the book's website at www.whenhelpingworks.org

Preface

THIS BOOK IS ABOUT the impact of negative stereotype threat in intercultural contexts of global missions, humanitarian efforts, and how such an everyday predicament infringes on people's performance due to fears and anxious reactions about confirming negative stereotypes about identity, abilities, and effectiveness. Stereotype threat happens when caricatures and negative understandings about people's identities are invoked. To this end, as I write this book the world is faced with numerous humanitarian challenges, about refugee migration in particular. There seem to be levels of discontent, fears, and anxieties that are driving inquiry into whom the refugees are and where they are coming from. Questions range from what is the right response to their plight and suffering, to how should they be treated and whether or not they are objects of charity, terror, Trojan horses, or possible allies. The reactions to such issues vary from sea to shining sea, across cultures and regions.

I was particularly intrigued by the response of one hundred religious leaders in the United States who wrote to the president and his administration in defiance of his executive orders signed to temporarily restrict and suspends refugee admission to the United States. In a CNN op-ed, the Christian leaders and pastors wrote, "As Christians, we have a historic call expressed over two thousand years, to serve the suffering. We cannot abandon this call now." But what about the hardships that tend to bubble in intercultural engagements and dynamics due to the multiple challenges to be encountered by both the newcomers and the host culture? Is it enough to be committed to receiving the new travelers without preparing for the enactment of corrective intercultural sensibilities?

Over the many years, I have worked internationally and interacted with people from around the world. I have also been fortunate to teach and consult on matters of intercultural communication, community engagement, humanitarian work, global studies, and global missions with various groups and organizations. I have realized that there are well-intended people with convictions who volunteer and participate in intercultural contexts, yet in their own acknowledgments and admissions, the limitations of their "good intentions" are not lost on them. Their levels of preparedness are found wanting of various perspectives. This book attempts to contribute to the discussion on readiness. In so doing, I provide a positive and corrective perspective about the love ethic of helping neighbor, which is in contrast to a particular mind-set's attempts to scapegoat and marginalize the art of helping, at the expense of redressing some of the core issues of identity I raised in the book.

For many of the students I have interacted with regarding intercultural intelligence at various universities, there is a desire to learn the helpful ways to dispel negative stereotypes about the places and people they want to visit and work in. Other people want to help through giving their time, and material and financial resources, but they find themselves preoccupied with the loftiness of the challenge of interculturality before them. If you are seeking to understand some of the tricky dimensions of participating in intercultural engagement and work as you reflect on people's lives and your identity in the quest to demonstrate intercultural mindfulness, this book is for you.

Introduction

You Should Help!

We [might not be able] to help everyone, but everyone can help someone

FROM AN ELDERLY HOMELESS LADY'S CARDBOARD SIGN, AMERICA

HAVE YOU FELT CONTROLLED by opinions about the idea of helping people and the thought of how you will be perceived because of helping the poor? What might be at the core of such dynamics? Are you a Christian from anywhere to everywhere who is afraid of helping the "poor" for fear of hurting them? This book insists that stereotype threat-based perceptions affect Christians' self-concepts, perceptions of others, and performance in intercultural missions. This is due to fears and anxious reactions about confirming negative stereotypes about their identity, abilities, and effectiveness.Stereotype threat happens when caricatures and negative understandings about people's identities are invoked. To this end, you might even feel immobilized and terrified of making the wrong decisions despite your convictions and good intentions to help people who are in need. Helping people is an integral characteristic of people of faith. However, there is a rising tide of a get-tough attitude in global missions that is set on stigmatizing the ministry of helping the resource poor. Yet, when you consider who exactly are labeled "the poor," you will be intrigued with what you find. Suffice it to note that instead of embracing a spiritual high road of love, kindness, and generosity; virtues that are consistent with the attitude of Christ, factors that are not to be confused with the dysfunctional behavior of blind enabling, get-tough mentality, and comission that stands to cripple Christian communities of faith involved in global missions.

Have you been told that helping people in hardship will hurt them? In this book, I will discuses the predictable levels of such claims and how they undermine the ministry of hospitality and generosity. The voices against the idea of helping without strings attached want you to castigate your intentions as flimsy desires of stereotypic "do gooders," all the while encouraging you to adopt intentions based on disengagement infested with fear, anxiety, and false guilt. They postulate an overly confident demeanor of their ability to fix and deliver on their self-congratulating perception for the scary "other," only to be rudely awakened by the negligence of their own imperfections.

With some of the good that can be modestly realized in short-term mission, does going on short-term trips for the duration of one, two, or three weeks in Uganda, Kenya, Haiti, or Guatemala make you an expert on the lives of the local people? How naively predictable does a person have to be to assume to be an expert of Africans or Africa just because you hold a generalist major in "African studies"?

This discussion will argue for a robust intercultural and action-based dialogue as an alternative to a one-directional and negative mind-set that fosters stereotype threat in global missions. When you fail to ask the right questions while helping anyone who has fallen on hard times (and helping is a positive spiritual virtue), you are prone to be fixated and act based on your systemic assumptions and negative stereotypes about who they are. In fact, as a prelude litmus test, you can even take some time to ask yourself about your beliefs about who the poor are and what your stereotypes about what the poor are like. Then reflect on the fact that the poor come in all shapes, colors, forms, and sizes. Case in point, a usually mute and interesting fact about the poor in the United States, which is the richest country in the world, is that they tend to be religious. According to a 2010 Gallup poll, there is a convincingly positive correlation between steady adherence to spirituality, faith, and privation.[1] Where can you find these people? The *New York Times* journalist Alan Flippen explains that the most poverty-stricken places in the United States are the ten lowest counties in the country, which include a cluster of six in the Appalachian Mountains of eastern Kentucky along with four others in various parts of the rural South[2] and other places in the country. Some of the poorest populations can also be

---

1. Crabtree, "Religiosity Highest."
2. Flippen, "Where Are the Hardest Places to Live."

found in the majority world. Even though the Gallup poll provides evidence of an association between religiosity and deprivation in society, causal factors are absent. The problem of poverty also seems to be largely associated with the social identity of "minority" groups. Ann Lin and David Harris in their book, *The Colors of Poverty*, note that "the hardship of poverty falls disproportionately on ethnic minorities and female-headed households."[3] The generality of negative stereotypes concerning the poor have both a local and global reach and carry over in global missions. When missions are influenced by an individual's negatively stereotypical worldview, there will be irrational promotions of confusion, fear, and anxiety among followers of Jesus who are seeking to participate in God's mission in the global church. This attitude is evident in some of the literature available on global missions in the Christian book market.

Global missions are experiencing interesting dynamics. We live in a very fortunate time where the world has access to information about the boom of Christianity and an increasing excitement about missions through short-term trips. According to the Gordon-Conwell Theological Seminary's *International Bulletin of Missionary Research*, the number of worldwide Christians in the year 1900 was 558,131,000, then 2,419,221,000 in 2015, and the number of worldwide Christians is projected to increased to 3,437,236,000 by 2050.[4] This is encouraging news and a testament to the effect of God's love and the gospel in global missions. From a global missions and international church partnerships perspective, imagine what followers of Christ could accomplish as a united front in the great commandment (Matt 12:30–31, 22:36–40; Luke 10:27) and the great commission (Matt 28:18–20; John 17:18, 20:21).

Currently, there are many books that are increasingly discussing the idea of helping the needy in both local and global missions amidst the changing climate of globalization, socioeconomic uncertainty, and geopolitical instability of the twenty-first century. In the process, many believers are facing a paralyzing fog propelled by certain Western evangelical global missions experts who prescribe various mission methods. Increasingly, among Christian evangelical circles in the Western world, a growing concern pervades the discussion about the role of Christians from the Western church in global missions and Christian humanitarian work. The questions on the minds of contemporary Western missions-minded churches are: What is the

3. Lin and Harris, *Colors of Poverty*, 54.
4. Gordon-Conwell Theological Seminary, "Christianity 2015," 29.

role of the "global North church" in global missions? Are Western Christians doing more harm than good? How should Christians from the West participate in helping? These questions and more are of particular relevance to the discussion in this book because they have been appropriated by a prevailing mind-set of a one-directional mission model that obstructs and obscures the ministry of helping in global missions. — *mutual giving + receiving*

Of particular concern to me is the new mind-set that is increasingly popularized in the book *When Helping Hurts: How to Alleviate Poverty Without Hurting The Poor—And Yourself* by Brian Fikkert and Steve Corbett. This book is becoming the "bible" and guiding principles for Western missiological institutional and personal strategies to non-Western communities across the world. The likelihood of people to follow different visions in missions is not uncommon. In fact, in this technologically interconnected, informational, and knowledge-based twenty-first century, I am willing to posit that oppositional views in global mission will grow louder. I have no doubt that Fikkert and Corbett are well-endowed in their fields of expertise, even kind and caring individuals. However, I believe that they have an inconsiderate and misleading concept. How could they hurriedly miss the clues? Are they so set in their preconceptions and perceptions of people who do not look or act like them, that not even their technical elitism could alleviate their overconfidence? The mind-set they promote encourages and mobilizes Christians in the Western world to participate in poverty alleviation, but from a place of fear, anxiety, false guilt, dominance, and therefore a negative stereotypic perspective. For example, Fikkert and Corbett write,

> We are grieved when we see churches using poverty alleviation strategies . . . that violate "best practice" methodologies developed by theorists and practitioners over the course of many decades.[5]

A timely question is: who's "best practice" and for whom? At face value, the above statement portrays a level of concern for a sort of ill-conceived missions approach in the Western church toward the majority world cultural contexts. Yet it is not difficult to witness the fact that Fikkert and Corbett still function and suffer from a mind-set encumbered by an unbiblical attitude and fallacy of "the best to the rest" in global missions. Here is an instance of the law of unintended consequences—a case of well-intended American missionaries, their values, and their assumptions that reestablish the problems they seek to decry and alleviate in the first place. In

---

5. Fikkert and Corbett, *When Helping Hurts*, 14.

championing such thought processes unwittingly, the authors race for the center in order to dictate to the people on the "periphery." As one repatriated US missionary from Africa, Nik Ripken, put it, "Though our motives are not always suspect, we generally come and tell other people to 'sit down and listen' while we stand and speak. . . . We are the 'haves,' and they are the 'have-nots.'"[6]

Fikkert and his mate establish a purely stereotypically subjective, pietistic, and rather technocratic strategy mediated with power trips over the categorical "them," consequently knitting a threat-ridden trap for their imaginary clients. Both the givers in missions from the "North American Church" and the recipients of missions in the metaphorical Global South live under this threat. Isn't it rather reasonable, instead, to elevate an attitude that encourages the practice of mutuality (John 17; 1 Cor 8:13–15), love, helpfulness, and commitment to a united global church which seeks the Kingdom of God together? In the chapters ahead I will reflect more on such alternatives.

In the meantime, I am struck by Fikkert and Corbett's assumption, which they portray as grievances over the perceived lack of what they term "best practices" in global missions. More so, their audacity to elevate themselves as representatives of the represented, namely the total voice for the global church, is doubtful. In my view, their "grievances" are based in fear and anxiety and are driven by false guilt. Granted, the grievances could be culturally relevant to them, but they do not represent the Ugandan context. The outlook they present maintains and promotes a top-down higher rank view of the Western missionary expatriate identity, while furthering the negative stereotypic and low view of the ordinary person from the majority world. Fikkert acknowledges that he is from a community of fourth generation Dutch immigrants and is an upper class Presbyterian, but does he speak for all?[7]

Out of bewilderment for some of their readers' reactions to their work, the authors lament about some of the responses to their book, noting that it is unfortunate for them to know that some readers say they are not quite sure what to do next. Their readers want to help but they are not sure how to get started after reading Fikkert and Corbett's work. Some have even said that they feel a bit paralyzed, being so worried about doing harm that they are afraid to help at all.[8]

6. Ripken, "What's Wrong."
7. Fikkert and Corbett, *When Helping Hurts*, 21.
8. Ibid., 14.

I remain curiously concerned as to why such a paralyzing fear struck the North Americans and missions-minded Christians whom Fikkert and Corbett claimed to address. Fear is a common emotion to all human beings and happens across cultures. Yet how is it that believers who are called to live in the ways of God's love (John 10:101; 2 Tim 1:7; 1 John 4:18) are reading literature on missions that induces and uses fear and defeating panic as a motivational factor? Why such fear and confusion? The Scriptures make it clear that "God is not a God of confusion but of peace. As in all the churches."[9]

Something about this kind of fear and distress requires normative reasoning and dialogue with the input of ethnically diverse voices from the totality of the global church. Along with this shift away from empathy toward a self-preserving mind-set in global missions comes the confusion of saying one thing and doing another. Global short- and long-term missions activities have become permeated with fear that commands devotees to refrain from doing "things for people that they can do for themselves."[10] Unfortunately, even though such a slogan sounds enticing, it is an oversimplification of how people experience suffering. The subcontext of such sloganeering stands the risk of propelling well-meaning Western Christians to adopt an attitude of, "I'll keep what is mine," all the while saying to people in need, the very people missionaries are called help, "You are on your own." This leads to the denial of practicing the biblical principle of "from everyone who has been given much, much will be demanded; and from the one who has been entrusted with much, much more will be asked."[11] How simplistic does one have to be to think that they can know the complexities surrounding people's need on a short-term mission trip? There is an assumption that Western missionaries, are intelligent enough to know the needs of the poor better from a distance than the poor themselves know of their own pain and situation. Such a mind-set tends to vacillate from abject ignorance to abject certainty about people groups and their cultural contexts. In your everyday reality you do things for people all the time. For your mothers, sisters, pastors, spouse, neighbors, friends, and country out of love. If you take some time to see how people in Uganda love to share the little they have in most of the village and homes, you'll see what I mean. When I think of that kind of generosity, I am also reminded of the story of the widow who gave "out of her poverty, put in everything—all she had to live on."[12] Wow, what a

9. 1 Cor 14:33.

10. Fikkert and Corbett, *When Helping Hurts*, 109.

11. Luke 12:48.

12. Mark 12:44.

servant leader! During my childhood in Uganda, I remember how my father would buy foodstuffs in pairs. One day I asked him why he did it that way, his answer: "One is for our neighbor." To this day I still marvel at such an attitude. So, people are always doing things out of love even for people who are able to do certain things for themselves, it's just that certain challenges require a helping hand up no matter one's abilities.

Why would you not act out of love for the people that God has called you to be with in community and to befriend, especially those of the household of the faith?[13] Why promote the fear of the "other"? In all matters of fairness and cordiality, Fikkert and Corbett's book serves the benefit of a much-needed conversation of global proportions regarding Christian missions. However, I feel that even though their perspective is not due to maliciousness, it is chronically flawed and is in fact harmful to the very people they are intending to help and guide: both the "giver" and the "receiver" and visa versa in Western evangelical churches.

In the absence of a clear and articulate alternative to the deleterious omissions and distortions to helping in the ubiquitous and recent mind-set on missions exemplified in Fikkert and Corbett's proposals, many people in Western evangelicalism lend themselves to limiting and harmful processes. This book presents another view. What's the nature of the helping ministry I propose in global missions? One not of simple solutions, but one that holds to biblical love and unity. Without this, global missions become a difficult and thorny path to traverse.

Let me note that this is not an entire review on Fikkert and Corbett's book, and I refer to their material as an example of the greater infiltrating outlook of this particular mind-set in missions today. There is a need to ensure that the global church (John 17; Rom 12:5; Eph 4:12–16, 25) is faithfully represented and soundly equipped with tools for good works of helping to the glory of God (Prov 31:1–9; Jer 22:3; Mark 12:30–31). This is in line with biblical scriptures about giving (1 John 1:15–20; Prov 3:27; Jas 2:15–16). It is my conviction that there is only one global church (John 17:21; 2 Cor 5:18, 20; Eph 1:9–10, 2:13–16; Col 1:20, 3:11) and it is the only solution for helping people in healthy ways to promote generosity, love that casts out fear, and declaring good news. This requires the breaking down of fear-based barriers and negative stereotypic perspectives that exist in the arena of global missions, while faithfully following the words and way of Jesus and the traditions of the historical church.

13. Heb 6:10; Gal 6:10.

For over twenty years, I have been involved in the helping business, ever since the love of Jesus transformed my life. Coming from a socioeconomic and geopolitical background full of adversities and joy as well, I was fortunate to access a school education modeled after the British education system, which was delivered through colonialism in Uganda. I wore a uniform of shorts, shirt, at times a sweater, and knee-high socks to school. I experienced the ups and downs in the helping ministry, and the realities of war, displaced peoples, disease, poverty, orphans, vulnerable children, child soldiers, church planting, international government relations, festival evangelism, and building friendships across cultures.

This book discusses those experiences and how they are relevant to today's discussion and the practice of generosity, unity, peace, suffering, love, and redemption in global missions. This book is written on the conviction that these experiences and the questions they raise about the helping ministry are prevalent and relevant throughout the global church experience to date.

Chapter 1

To Give . . . or Not to Give . . .
That Is the Question

Facts are stubborn things; and whatever may be our wishes, our inclinations, or the dictates of our passions, they cannot alter the states of facts and evidence.

JOHN ADAMS[1]

MY FRIEND DAVE IS from England. Dave remembers when he realized he was very rich. He was working with a small UK Christian charity in Northern Thailand driving a pickup truck along a dusty dirt road in the stunning jungle mountains of the Thai/Myanmar border delivering rice, dried fish, oil, and chili to some of the refugee communities we were working with. The area was and still is surrounded by communities of displaced Shan people from Myanmar fleeing the long-standing persecution of ethnic groups by the military government. To avoid arrest, many families work in the fields by day for the smallest of wages and live in makeshift communities with limited access to basic provisions, health services, or education for their children. Families fear the authorities may exploit their vulnerable position by demanding bribes or may deport unregistered migrants back to the border. Which is a journey back to persecution.

At one of the first communities to which Dave came, a man led him to a frail, elderly woman in her bamboo home who was very sick with belly pain and had not eaten for days. Her family was clearly very fearful and anxious. What should he do? He had a vehicle; cash in his wallet, and legitimate papers to be living and working in Thailand and was standing face

---

1. Adams, *Biography in His Own Words*, 121–22.

to face with the woman with no vehicle, no cash in her wallet, and no legal papers to be in Thailand. She was in a lot of pain. This was in 2001.

In 1993 Dave became a Christian at the age of seventeen; he was propelled by God's love to help other people. At the age of eighteen he joined Youth With a Mission for Discipleship Training School, followed by the School of Frontier Missions, and became a missionary afterward. His journey to being on the Thai/Myanmar border road that day involved a myriad of learning and experiences: a three-month placement in Seville, Spain, with a Spanish church, a three-month placement in Kolhapur, India, working under an Indian pastor and his family, two years in China managing a project in a state-run orphanage, and three years of working with displaced communities in Northern Thailand. He met this lady and her family that day as he was delivering food to several of the families on the border. This meeting is not apart from a larger history because Dave was born and raised in England and she belonged to the Shan people group of Myanmar. It was the British government and its colonialist endeavors over sixty years ago that had created the military Burman government that had ousted her family from their family lands through persecution and forced dislocation across the border into Thailand. There was a broader historical context to our meeting. Their meeting was not without the prejudices, experiences, and stereotype perceptions that had shaped both of them. Yet, he had money, a vehicle, and other resources. She did not.

What was his excuse? Should he pause to pray about it and come back another day? Should he ask "what would Jesus do?" His response on that day was unequivocal. He placed the elderly lady inside the front of the truck with her family in the back and drove to the hospital in Fang. He walked into the patient admitting area, he handed over his driver's license, and told the hospital staff he was responsible for this family and the costs. A week later, after a successful surgery, they all drove back to her home with smiles on their faces thanking God for his loving kindness and continued waking up daily to life. Was that the right thing to do? Should he have helped? Another scenario is about Jane (that's not her real name). She was a university student at Makerere University, the largest university in Uganda, and my colleagues and I met her while doing community outreach work. She and her family contributed to her tuition at college.

However, a time came when she wasn't able to afford the fees she needed to graduate due to financial hardship. In Uganda, there isn't a federal student loan program like that in United States. Jane was hopeful that

God would provide for her need and she shared with a few friends about the remaining tuition she needed to graduate. One of her friends was my wife, Kristen, who was visiting in Uganda from the United States. Along with others, Kristen eagerly helped. Jane is a teacher, a mother, and is pursuing her goals in life. It's been close to fifteen years now; Jane and Kristen are longtime friends. Should Kristen have ignored Jane's challenge and left it up to Jane's Ugandan friends, resisting the opportunity to help because Kristen was an "outsider"?

Let me introduce a different story, close to a decade later, in another context on the Isle of Wight in England, over five thousand miles away from Fang. In 2009, Mark Wells was walking home one night when he fell head first into a storm drain yards from his house. All through the night he shouted, "Help me, help me, please," but neighbors were too frightened to help. Dismissed as a drunk by his neighbors, Mr. Wells was found dead in the morning as he had suffocated during the night. According to the newspaper article, the coroner did not blame residents for ignoring the thirty-two-year-old's cries, saying it was a "sad reflection on society that people were too scared to venture out of their homes when they heard screams," and that people are fearful and nervous about getting involved when faced with the reality of helping or not helping in a situation. Bill Fox, chairman of the conflict management training company Maybo stated that "the worst thing is to do nothing."[2]

It is very pertinent that this quote comes from a professional conflict management specialist, because conflict at many levels is a real issue of our time in global missions. Many people have developed an internal soul conflict about helping. We are fearful, we are confused, and many of us have experienced great pain in the process of helping and receiving help. Why? What has happened? In 2010, Dave and I facilitated a potential donor team from a US church. We were visiting an HIV clinic for children started by the NGO we were working for. It was late in the evening, the clinic was closed, and the hosting was over when a distraught girl came out of the village toward Dave while I was meeting with another group of people in the community. She was carrying her baby sister, a sick and limp child suffering from malaria. The parents had died from HIV/AIDS. Again, he had a vehicle, cash in his wallet, and yet . . . this time he did not help. Instead, he just prayed for the child.

---

2. Barkham, "Taking the Risk Out of Being a Good Samaritan."

Why did he not help?

According to Dave, he had become afraid to get involved. He had become confused about helping. He was a prime candidate for the bystander effect. Where would he take her? The clinic was closed. It was late at night. He was responsible for a team of western donors who needed to head back to the guesthouse. Why did he just not open his wallet and give her money? What had happened to him since 2001? He found himself with questions like: Should he give her money? Can he trust this person to use the money? Shouldn't she trust God for the money from her neighbors? Should he go and knock on the straw doors of the mud huts to corral the neighbors into giving money from local assets? I can guarantee you that if he had given the lady $20 or $50 from his wallet that within twenty-four hours that sick child would have been in the nearest best clinic in her district or in Kampala, the capital city of Uganda. (Generally, the closer a sick person can get to the larger cities, the better the health care.)

She would have used that money to find a bike, a truck ride, or a bus to get her sister the care she needed. In this instance, *not* helping definitely hurt. He discussed this story with a psychologist recently who suggested to him that were she in this situation she would have sat down with the girl and sick baby to help her understand what her problems really were and to understand why she was poor. It is understandable that she was coming from a clinic background; however, this is a case that required resource help at that given point in time and not just psychoanalytic tactics. The family needed money immediately, not questions. When a house is on fire do you stop to think about the possible cause of the fire, or do you call 911?

Dave would tell you there are many people he has met that he both has and has not helped. Indeed, it is the people he has not helped that he remembers most clearly. It is seared into his conscience, like a sinful occurrence. He would say he went against scripture (Jas 2:16; 1 John 3:17). Was helping in Fang and not helping in Uganda the right thing to do? According to Fikkert and Corbett's viewpoint, he should have stepped back, made sure he had the right policy, researched the community extensively, mobilized local assets and been aware of the "explicit guidelines or policies as to roles and authority [in the community], including what to do if the community members don't carry out their responsibilities."[3]

---

3. Fikkert and Corbett, *When Helping Hurts*, 163.

This may be the view in some development and technocratic circles, but the reality is not that clear-cut or well-set in the daily experience of the non-Western resource poor and even in the biblical understanding of generosity. Christians are called to a life of generosity in good times and in bad times, in season and out of season. As followers of Christ, we are called to participate in the good news.

> "If you see some brother or sister in need and have the means to do something about it but turn a cold shoulder and do nothing, what happens to God's love? It disappears. And you made it disappear."[4]

In the story of the aging lady in Fang, she was terribly sick and needed help. Was it proper for Dave to help out? Based on Scripture, I believe the answer is a resounding and non-negotiable *yes.* Dave should have helped and anyone in this position ought to do the same in global missions. Which begs the proverbial question "what would Jesus do?" Yet if one looked attentively to the Scriptures, it is apparent that a better reflection leads us to imagine Jesus asking, "What did I say, and based on my word, what are you going do?"[5]

Jesus said of the faithful and prepared servant, "For I was sick and you visited me."[6] Without debating which kind and what degree of sickness is deserving of attention and which is not, it is clear that Jesus invites his disciples and followers in the global church to respond to human deprivation. In all the Abrahamic faiths, there are practices that are dutiful for the adherents. For example, in Islam, the practice of charity to the poor is not a choice, it is obligatory. Jesus' dialogue with the wealthy local official who inquired, "Good teacher, what must I do to deserve eternal life"[7] is an invitation to sell everything he owned, give it all to the poor, and follow Jesus. Jesus' thoughts and response toward the needy are unequivocal, and therefore helping people as a gospel, solution-based response is not a pick-and-mix option for followers of Christ, but a matter of necessity. Therefore, the question is how, then, should we help in global missions, and where is the fear coming from? It is at this point that we must investigate the mind-set that is represented within Corbett and Fikkert's book *When Helping Hurts: How to Alleviate Poverty Without Hurting the Poor—And Yourself.*

4. 1 John 3:17.
5. 1 Pet 5:2.
6. Matt 25:36.
7. Luke 18:18.

The authors seem to have struck a particular preexisting mind-set within Western evangelical missiology, catching the attention of various notable Western evangelical leaders.

In a fashion of fairness and admiration for the author's audacity to stimulate a conversation about the potential challenges in missions and their suggestive solutions, I see the need to take seriously the distorted consequences of their body of work in the global church. Unfortunately, based on my life-long familiarity with life in Uganda and current involvement of working internationally, I find the culturally predetermined vision of "when helping hurts" problematic. It is within the opening introduction of *When Helping Hurts* where things go wrong and where a questionable and faulty foundation for the rest of the book is set for the reader. In unpacking this particular aspect in the following chapters I will demonstrate how promoting a negative stereotypical mind-set through a disrespectful descriptive narrative of the environment in which poor people live creates a prejudicial "us" and "them" barrier toward helping. For now, I focus on the story that Fikkert tells about his encounter with Elizabeth and Grace, whom Corbett and Fikkert in their opening setting identify as a "witch doctor" living in a community of people seeking refuge from humanitarian issues in Kampala, Uganda. We read about her conversion from witchcraft to Christ and also her story of battling with tonsillitis within a context of poverty and limited access to medicine and resources. Fikkert writes about going to visit Grace with Elizabeth, a local Kampala ministry leader, when Grace was absent from church due to sickness.

> After about a ten-minute walk, we entered Grace's one-room shack. Grace was lying on a mat on the dirt floor and writhing in agony. A plate with a few morsels of food covered with fleas was the only other thing in the place. Grace could not lift her head and could barely whisper. Elizabeth bent over and got close to try to understand Grace's faint words. Elizabeth then stood up and explained the situation to me. Grace had developed tonsillitis. Because she is poor and has HIV, the local hospital refused to treat her. Desperate for relief, Grace paid her neighbor to cut out her tonsils with a kitchen knife. "We are in the very bowels of hell," I thought to myself.[8]

Fikkert was faced with the choice to help Grace . . . or not to help. He chose to help and gave the $8 needed for the lifesaving penicillin to heal Grace

---

8. Fikkert and Corbett, *When Helping Hurts*, 23–24.

and she was on the road to health and well-being in no time. But the story does not end there. Fikkert initially feels happy about his helping efforts, but under self doubt, fear, anxiety, and false guilt on the plane journey home he descended in a crisis and conflict:

> Suddenly, I felt sick. . . . Yes, [Pastor] Elizabeth and I had led the witch doctor to Christ and had saved her life. But I suddenly realized that we might have done an enormous amount of harm in the process.[9]

Fikkert is concerned that as the visiting American within Uganda, giving money had harmed the local church congregation, the refugee community who were enrolled in his small business class, and it had harmed Grace herself. It is this conclusion that forms the basis for writing the book *When Helping Hurts* to explore this tension and uncertainty.

Fikkert's consent to buy the lifesaving medicine for Grace was the right thing to do, but why does he insist that he was the wrong person to do so? Should he be applauded for a heroic discovery? What is going on here? Whose principles does he violate by helping? Does this strike you as odd? Plus, is it possible to feel sick or ashamed because "he helped"? Isn't that what Christians do—help those in need?

As a Western academic, he is more concerned about violating the Western-grown, asset-based community development principles, rather than embracing and acknowledging the call to the helping ministry? According to Fikkert, it was the local pastor, church, small business class participants, and refugee community that should have been responsible for the problem he faced and helped out their own.

> The truth is that there was more than enough time to walk back to the church, where the small-business class was still assembled, and ask the participants what they could do to help Grace. While the refugees were extremely poor, they could have mustered the eight cents per person to help pay for the penicillin. In short, I had violated . . . key elements of [asset-based community development].[10]

Fikkert suddenly turns from being generous, to regret, wishing he could recall his gift in order to authoritatively make those extremely poor African refugees provide the $8 needed to treat the elderly woman instead of giving it himself. He collapses into himself and resorts to an argument

9. Ibid., 25.
10. Ibid.

for self-preservation and self interest with the fear of hurting himself at the expense of encouraging generosity in global missions. In his estimate, there is something off with these Africans. Why aren't they responsible and caring? Fikkert's lack of willingness to be vulnerable is usurped by a desire to appear as the Western foreigner equipped with the intellectual shrewdness to "best discover" for these Africans their role in their culture; led him to assume and promote the worst about the Africans present, that they wouldn't come to the rescue of their kinfolk. However, how about the positive possibility that they are already mustering their scarce financial resources to help other people, aside from that single incident. It's now simply Fikkert's turn to demonstrate love and show kindness. Instead, he wishfully concocts a bystander's mission strategy for the Western church to practice in the majority world. An approach that restricts generosity, heightens anxiety and promotes the release of the stress chemical in the body called cortisol, which also inhibits empathy. That's how and when not helping hurts. As a Ugandan, I find Fikkert's conclusion off, because the mind-set he is promoting is based on negative and wrong assumptions. He was shackled in selfish bias that appears to put his interests before others while becoming a conduit for stereotype threat. Paul instructs, "Do nothing out of selfish ambition or vain conceit. Rather, in humility value others above yourselves, not looking to your own interests but each of you to the interests of the others."[11]

What does it cost him or any Western missionary by helping a poor sick lady? There is no harm in doing this kind of good deed of helping. What is the personal conundrum for Fikkert that forms the basis for most of his book and the greater get-tough mind-set toward the needy he encourages in global missions? It is as though Fikkert and anyone who embraces such advances, remain convinced that giving to people who are not Westerners while on missions violates Western-generated development principles that supersede biblical mandates about helping. What have missions come to? Of what use is Fikkert if he only values the observance of Western etiquette over helping and demonstrating the love of God? If Fikkert had not given the money, would Grace have died like Mark Wells? Was Fikkert not a member of the community at that short-term point, given that he was living in Kampala on sabbatical, ensconced in relationships with Elizabeth and others in the community? Giving in Uganda is a relational experience where both the giver and receiver experience the cheerful effects of happiness.

11. Phil 2:3–4.

Again, only not helping is the problem. Had God led him there to not give? I guarantee you that the same Ugandans from whom the American missionary advises fellow Westerners to withhold their resources, are the same people on who he was dependent for cultural help and resourcefulness. How come that didn't hurt Fikkert?

I am sure that $8 as a ratio of his daily income was much smaller than eight cents of the refugee community member's daily income. Although the Ugandan pastor's perspective and attempts to comfort Fikkert failed to register, Fikkert would have been served well to reflect on the encouragement from Scripture. According to the book of 1 John,

> By this we know love, that he laid down his life for us and we ought to lay down our lives for our brothers. But if anyone has the world's goods and sees his brother in need, yet closes his heart against him, how does God's love abide in him? Little children, let us not love in word or talk but in deed and in truth.[12]

Let me take you back to the story in Fang at the beginning of this chapter for a moment. Shortly after the events of the initial story above, Dave was facilitating another short-term missions team from England. They were serving with Health and Nutritional Development Services and driving them to the community center where they would serve for a few months. After making the introductions to the Thai and Shan staff he left the non-Thai speaking team to get accustomed to their new home and he began the long drive back to Chiang Mai. He arrived home late at night and received a phone call early in the morning from the team in Fang. One of the English girls had fallen sick in the night with belly pain. The excellent community center staff took care of her and drove her to a Fang hospital, where she had her appendix removed through open surgery. Who was the good samaritan this time? The poor helped the wealthy with all they could.

Dave and I have been blessed to sit with families in some of the most materially lacking communities: Oddar Meanchey in Northern Cambodia, Northwest Uganda, outside Port-au-Prince, Haiti, and the island of Nias in Indonesia . . . and the list continues. In every single circumstance the families we've met, have provided a feast of the best food they have, providing a great banquet for the guest, and we ate together. Most of the people we have met living with very little know how to give and give generously.

---

12. 1 John 3:16–19.

When Helping Hurts is a fear-inducing title that proceeds to take the reader on a journey of the analysis of poverty and helping that presents many with lopsided methodological approaches on a variety of topics. My chief concern is that the content and conclusions cause more confusion than clarity for people considering helping within the global arena of the missions. As I read the book, the content does not align with my experiences of living in Uganda and the time I have spent in other countries around the world. The content is also disparate from my experience as a Ugandan national who has worked with missionaries and organizations from all walks of life. Fikkert's work has muddied the water of missiology by further entrenching negative stereotype threat about people in the majority. His trend of thought encourages anti-helping and anti-generosity sentiments.

Have we systematized the process of giving to a fault, so much that when we come face to face with a person in need, we do not know how to freely and cheerfully give? In my view, Fikkert's advice to Western Christians is a dangerous weed of confusion. This is contrary to the Scriptures, since they clearly note, "For God is not a God of disorder but of peace—as in all the congregations of the Lord's people."[13]

We use phrases like "empowering the poor," "leading from behind," "do no harm," and "give a voice to the voiceless" without understanding the implications of these phrases from a gospel viewpoint. These are some of the phrases I would like to unpack. When God places you in a location where you meet people in need, is he inviting you to participate through compassion and generosity to meet that need as well? Or is he asking you to be less concerned about it, look the other way, and let someone else meet that need? My own story is evidence of the fearless and joyful outcomes of giving and receiving.

When I was fourteen years old living in Kampala, Uganda, my father lost his accountant job due to changes that were going on in the East African nation as many government programs were changing according to World Bank structural adjustments and privatization. I had to drop out of school because my parents could no longer pay the fees. At that time parents had to pay for their child to go to school; there was no free education available.

If parents or guardians did not keep up with payments, then the children were called out in class, humiliated amongst their peers and sent out of school labeled as "school fees defaulters." I used to sneak back in because education meant learning and acquiring skills, and was the best

13. 1 Cor 14:33.

opportunity gateway for building any hope for the future and to participate in the economy in a meaningful way. We all knew that children who went through education all the way to earn a college degree generally earn more and have a better life. I used to slip back into class with the hopes that I would not be detected or that a different teacher would be on duty, praying that somehow a miracle would help me. Getting kicked out for the second time in the same day would be so painful. When that happened I would sit on a hill outside the school to listen to what the teachers were saying and take some notes. Even then, the teachers would look through the window into the outside of the school compound and chase us away because we had not paid for the lessons.

For three years I was a school fees drop out and labeled as such. For many months I would stay inside the home, because people who knew me knew I was supposed to be in school, and having to explain why I was not was painful. It had social ramifications for my family, for me, and it carried a negative stigma of no fault of my own, against my will and wishes, and through no fault of my mother or father as well. It was so painful for us all.

Because of the stigma attached to this social identification of non-school attendees, my brothers, sisters, and I were forced to disengage from the pain and become isolated because of the stereotype attached to us as poor. When you are struggling economically and living in abject poverty, life is painful.

For me, it was not just that my status was gone, it fed into a larger discourse of history and Christianity. For countries that were colonized, Christianity came as a package of three C's from the colonizers: commerce, civilization, and Christianity. Education was introduced as the viable on-ramp to the highway of the good life found in the three C's. Therefore, not having access to the three C's due to our non-school fees identity, the on-ramp was taken away from us through no fault of our own. Even as a follower of Christ, to be now outcasts, all of these elements sent us into existential crises that caused us to question the very meaning of life.

I used to ask people I knew, relatives, friends, to help me with some money to get back into school, but they did not have money to give. I devised a strategy to market myself as a child needing school and tried to fundraise for my school. I even got some jobs but the jobs did not pay enough to get me to school, only to get to the job and back by public transport. That was only when I got paid; in fact, there were numerous days, due to the business struggling for revenue, where I wasn't paid and would walk to work nonetheless.

The street term for such transportation was "footsubishi," a spin-off of the motorcar Mitsubishi. I guess that was our way of making humor lemonade out of the bitter lemons of abject poverty. Oh, abject poverty and its stigma really hurts, I wouldn't wish it on anyone. Most of the time there were no jobs and when working I was thankful for something to do. In non-minimum-wage economies you get what you get, and how should I navigate the child labor issue? I was a child; I needed to be, and should have been, in school.

Society believes that by definition a person with a stigma is not quite human. Erving Goffman in his book *Stigma: Notes on the Management of Spoiled Identity* asserts, "on this assumption, we exercise varieties of discrimination, through which we effectively, if not unthinkingly, reduce [a person's] life chances."[14] During this period of time the ebb and flow of life itself continued for our family within this non-school-fee-dropout existence. We got sick, we got well, we found jobs, the jobs ended, we celebrated together, we mourned together. At times, help came in fits and starts, all credit to my father and mother who remained committed to our education throughout. Dropping in and out of school was part and parcel of life, and education was very inconsistent. From a place of a lack of resources and unable to go to class, I was compelled by the New Testament to proclaim the good news of Jesus in our community out of no expectation of gain but in obedience to God alone. The apostle Paul states,

> Still, I want it made clear that I've never gotten anything out of this for myself, and that I'm not writing now to get something. I'd rather die than give anyone ammunition to discredit me or impugn my motives. If I proclaim the Message, it's not to get something out of it for myself. I'm compelled to do it, and doomed if I don't! If this was my own idea of just another way to make a living, I'd expect some pay. But since it's not my idea but something solemnly entrusted to me, why would I expect to get paid? So am I getting anything out of it? Yes, as a matter of fact: the pleasure of proclaiming the Message at no cost to you. You don't even have to pay my expenses![15]

I would visit Makerere University so often that people thought I was a student, even while I was a high school drop out. In a place of lack of financial and material resources, God compelled me to be giving of my time and energy and myself relationally as the gospel educated me. The Spirit of God

---

14. Goffman, *Stigma*, 5.

15. 1 Cor 9:15–18.

sustained me as I found myself teaching the gospel from the Scriptures out of my resource poverty. But I desperately needed money. I needed help. No one had money to help. The university students, my family, my friends—there were no financial assets in the community.

Most of the university students were there because their parents had sold the family goats and small plots of land and produce from their gardens. The students had no goats to sell. There were no assets. One particular night, faced with broken dreams and the stigma of my predicament, I went home and my hope to go to school was so low that during my prayers before bed I crawled up into our dark room where we had no electricity and with tears streaming down my face I turned to the wall and begged God to take me back to school.

Everyday I had to answer the question from the university students who I was preaching to, "You are a young man, why are you not at school?" I begged God to one day allow me to go to university like the people I was proclaiming the gospel among. I saw that it was so important that I also studied. Being among university students really sharpened my desire for school.

It was in this context that God led Kevin and I to meet. Kevin, who was from the state of Georgia in the United States, was a missionary on a six-month placement with a certain organisation. I was assigned by the leadership of our church as Kevin's go-to guy for anything he needed help with culturally or logistically during his stay. That is where our friendship began. Whatever Kevin ate, I ate; wherever he stayed, I stayed. Kevin joined me at the university sharing the good news, and we became ministry partners. According to the Bible, when Jesus was "calling the Twelve to him, he began to send them out two by two and gave them authority over impure spirits."[16] I never purposely told Kevin about my education need for the fear of being stigmatized further, and primarily because God had given me a newly found joy with sharing the gospel at Makerere University.

In short time, Kevin self-discovered my education situation and needs through his own investigation. Eventually I had to tell him, "Actually I am a drop out. I want to go to school but I don't have the money." I remember the look on his face, he was devastated and he said, "Look, Michael, if there is anyone who has a bright future and is gifted, anyone who wants and deserves to go to school, it is you." Two days after that he brought his missionary support money, enough for a year's worth of school, and he said, "I cannot live with myself if I don't give you this money, let me know if

16. Mark 6:7; Luke 10:1.

you need more and anything else." This money was his missionary support money. He was giving and investing sacrificially.

God provided the on-ramp to the good life of education on that day. Helping did not hurt there. Giving was not complicated. Since that day, God sustained my education through high school in Kampala, university studies in the United States, the United Kingdom, and Hong Kong, and all the way through to recently completing my doctoral studies and continuing in post-doctoral research. The good life is happening to me. I am a happily married husband, I am a father, and I'm working toward this story happening for other people in Africa, through discipleship and practical leadership development, giving and helping lovingly in ways that work. Should Kevin have given the money? You tell me.

Kevin is a bright example of the generosity and compassion I personally admire about the passion for philanthropy in the United States. In fact, Alexis de Tocqueville lays my feelings out best when he notes, "Americans make associations to give entertainments, to found seminaries, to build inns, to construct churches, to diffuse books, to send missionaries to the antipodes; in this manner they found hospitals, prisons, and schools."[17] Kevin's ministry of helping and giving money in response to need can never be a culprit in any given locally and global context. How is it that a certain mind-set finds it acceptable to peddle unfounded fears about helping? For example, Fikkert's regret about spending $8 on medicine for a lady infected by HIV/AIDS with tonsillitis living in a slum is unfounded. In Fikkert's words, "I later realized I might have done an enormous amount of harm to St. Luke's Church and its pastor, to the refugees in the small-business class, and even to Grace herself."[18] It is here where I must outline my core concerns about the insensitive mind-set represented by Corbett and Fikkert and other proponents of the current near-sighted strategies in global missions. The fear- and anxiety-based indifference to giving of "West to the Rest" missiological efforts is deconstructive to the Gospel of Jesus Christ (2 Tim 1:7).

The way a person handles the decision of "to give or not to give," especially when the means to help are available, can be directly tied to how a person views oneself in relation to the other. The identity of the giver and how the giver views the person in need of help is crucial to whether or not people are helped at all. Fear, suspicion, anxiety, confusion, and control have become too commonplace in the helping ministry. I have encountered

17. Tocqueville, quoted in Boyer et al., *Enduring Vision*, 277.

18. Fikkert and Corbett, *When Helping Hurts,* 130.

a number of both short- and long-term missionaries involved in Christian humanitarian aid who are preoccupied with worries of whether to help or not to help.

It is clear to me that there is an irregularity of stereotype threat that dictates how people in global missions relate to one another and it has an impact of enormous proportions in communities. From this kind of everyday predicament, many questions arise. Are you doing the right thing by helping the poor? Perhaps a "messiah" complex motivates you? Are you helping people to feel self-righteous about yourself? Who deserves help and who does not deserve help? Are you worthy of helping one another? Can you even avoid helping?

Chapter 2

Unmasking Fear, Anxiety, and
False Guilt in Giving

The world is like a Mask dancing. If you want to see it well, you do not stand
in one place.

CHINUA ACHEBE

Do not be anxious about anything, but in every situation, by prayer and peti-
tion, with thanksgiving, present your requests to God.

PHIL 4:6

IN MANY MEETINGS WITH missions-minded folk, I have experienced warning signs that can so easily elude the mindfulness of the Christian evangelical community. In my view, the majority of people who are interested in
local and global missions, long and short term, have read the book *When
Helping Hurts* and are very quick to whip out the red warning card of "don't
help too much, you might hurt someone."

For example, my friend Dave was recently scouting a Christian school
for his children to attend and the dean of students sang high praise about
how the book shapes the new agenda of the high school mission teams for
Bible class. I was talking to a pastor who leads a large congregation who, in
his words, told me that reading *When Helping Hurts* fearfully "destroyed him"
as he lamented on his historical helping efforts while on missions trips and
the confusion he felt about helping people. I was taken aback by the effect of
fear in his life. What a negative impact! Is he going to help anyone anymore?

As the leader of his congregation, what will his church's local and global missions strategy look like? Hopefully it will be healthy, since in Africa when discussing matters of leadership, there is a proverbial understanding that "the fish rots from the head."

I wonder what kind of effect this mind-set propagated by Fikkert and Corbett is having on the entire mission machine and community here in America. Fikkert's troubling misrepresentation of life in Uganda and Ugandans surely isn't and should not be a moral motivation for how to do mission anywhere. So how can such problematic worldviews be prescribed for God's missions? Any adherence toward such mentalities are signs that the Western missions machine is squeaking loudly because of fear, anxiety, and false guilt, and needs some serious attention. "Something felt,"[1] an anguish about helping, is eating away at the missions community and taking mission-minded people by storm away from Jesus' message and the Great Commission.

Believers are inevitably corralled into fear, anxiety, and a hunger for control—traits that are reminiscent of imperialist paradigms and the survival-of-the-fittest approach that plagued the historical expansion of Western Christendom. I have interacted with this mind-set immensely, and in many occasions these conversations and the confusion about missions and helping is loud. You can try it. For many, it has become difficult to understand where the prickly issues about the act of helping really exist. I don't believe that helping is the problem; there are other malfunctions promoted in the "when helping hurts" mind-set that need to be uncovered.

Fear and stereotype threat—remember Grace?

In chapter 1, I discussed the question of giving using real examples including my own experiences. With this chapter, I will focus on the example given in *When Helping Hurts*, which is a problematic formulation that frames the whole helping dilemma, all the while promoting attitudinal conditions of fear, anxiety, and false guilt in missions. Let us review the basics of Fikkert's interaction with Grace, the elderly sick lady with tonsillitis in need of $8 to buy medicine that would alleviate her immediate pain and sickness. Fikkert meets Grace as part of his monitoring of attendees at the small business training also attended by people from a refugee community. Grace is absent for a few days and Fikkert goes to her home with a local leader, Elizabeth, to find her. Grace is very sick and in need of medication and Fikkert gives $8 for

1. LeDoux, *Anxious*, 4.

this cause. It is on the return journey home where he feels sick with guilt for helping Grace, believing that his helping hurt Grace, the refugees, and the community at large in Uganda. It is from this scenario that his book title and major theory emerge. In Fikkert's own words:

> Suddenly I felt sick. . . . Yes, [Pastor] Elizabeth and I had led the witch doctor to Christ and had saved her life. But I suddenly realized that we might have done an enormous amount of harm in the process.[2]

He concludes that

> the truth is that there was more than enough time to walk back to the church, where the small-business class was still assembled, and ask the participants what they could do to help Grace. While the refugees were extremely poor, they could have mustered the eight cents per person to help pay for the penicillin. In short, I had violated . . . key elements of [asset-based community development].[3]

Fikkert's idea of what he terms "the truth" is severely problematic. Instead of rejoicing about Grace's access to HIV/AIDS medicines, he slumps and regresses in wishing he, who had the means and was, moreover, a missionary, did not help. He wishes he had commanded the Africans who where mostly refugees to get with the program, put themselves together, and act responsibly. I have worked with refugees from Burundi, Rwanda, Sudan, and Congo in Uganda, and I attest that they don't need sympathy or missionary micro-managerial control; they need empathy, love, and partnership. They are kind people who care for each other, unlike Fikkert's negative rendering. They are most generous in their day-to-day demeanors, but they could still use help, especially from a wealthy person like Fikkert. When I first read his ominous superimpositions regarding perceived "hurt" in missions, I was curiously suspicious about his idea. As a Ugandan, I pondered on whether Fikkert finds it a novel idea that Africans, let alone those who are poor, can help each other. If so, what was Fikkert's mind-set before he met them? Did his "new epiphany" about the possibilities of Africans being generous to each other mean that he shouldn't help because otherwise his help hurts? What where his preconceived expectations? As I reflected on what Fikkert was saying, I realized that his premises about the people in Uganda who he claimed to help in his book were presumptuous. I believe a fact check is helpful here.

2. Fikkert and Corbett, *When Helping Hurts*, 25.
3. Ibid.

If the refugees he met were extremely poor, as he acknowledged, where does he suppose they would "muster" the eight cents from? On one hand, Fikkert admits that they are "extremely poor." In other words, they clearly don't have discretionary money or the metaphorical "boot straps." However, in the same breath Fikkert wishes he could have forced the "extremely poor" by promoting a missiological-based approach of "pull yourself up by your bootstraps." Fikkert definitely has not experienced abject poverty. Let me consider another scenario. What if the "extremely poor" African refugees did have boots or, say, sixty-six cents? I bet you that even if they had boots, they wouldn't be nearly as nice and expensive as the shoes on Fikkert's feet or most missionaries fresh off of the airplane. Don't even entertain the possibility of extra choices of shoes or "boots" piled up on shoe racks in your closet. It's a false socioeconomic appropriation. Most of the poor people in Uganda already share the little they have but they need help, too. Now in Uganda, there is a much better idiom that goes, "Pull up your socks." It applies in certain cases where, for example, school kids have school socks as part of their school uniforms. It is irrelevant, however, to poor children whose parent cannot afford to send them to school.

Where does Fikkert imagine that the "extremely poor" refugees will "muster" the discretionary money stashed away? Is he encouraging them to beg from other Ugandans? Even if they somehow had Fikkert's imaginary "eight cents," I guarantee you that the refugees would have spent that money on more pressing needs. Is Fikkert advocating that the poor be kicked when they are already hard pressed and economically down? Perhaps Fikkert wrongly assumes that they have steady jobs, they have extra to save underneath their pillows, and therefore all they need is barking and marching orders. He was also unaware that a wealthy visitor like him, through connecting with credible community leaders, can make tremendous relational and cultural inroads through generously giving to people's expressed needs. Now that's the real truth!

Unfortunately, Fikkert's case is a teachable moment of contextual myopia, which is convenient for an escapist logic that focuses on self-interest while promoting stereotype threats in missions. Does Fikkert want to be seen as benevolent toward the poor, and yet still prefers not to help out? Why the flight and need to resist the opportunity to help the poor in Africa? Think about what Fikkert is communicating about the people he met. It's as though he means to say that poor people in Africa are clean slates, easy to fix with prescriptive solutions based on a short-term trip. Sadly, he is promoting such a divisive and paternalistic idea to the Western evangelical community as a viable missiological mind-set. He also confirms the negative stereotype of Western missionaries as insensitive and burdened by a colonial mind-set. He unwittingly portrays Africans and refugees in this case as incompetent, uncaring, "always needy," and inherently lacking in intellect. In this way, Fikkert's idea is harmful to followers of Christ and missions in general. Worst of all, he is encouraging the production of a stereotype threat, a narrative mixed with negative stereotypes and cues that Western missionaries, Ugandans, Africans, and refugees will have to confront. Fikkert sets up many Western missionaries for a missiological and great commission experience based on a racial/ethnic imagination of difference. Western missionaries should not fall into the trap of becoming agents of negative stereotypes and priming a stereotype threat effect. A negative stereotype approach is not part of the great commission, but is in fact a great omission. I'll explain more about stereotype threat later.

Fikkert claims that he felt guilty for helping by giving money directly to someone with a screaming resource need, and he was fearful that his efforts caused pain. There is something terribly fateful and off with his logic. How bizarre, that helping caused pain for the person in need and the community at large? Where is the correlation and causation? Even if there was a correlation between Fikkert's help toward the poor, aging, and sick woman and the perceived pain (which there isn't), what is the cause of this pain he laments about?

I am not denying Fikkert's pain and in no way do I want to advocate for silence on his part. Yet what justifies his transference of the subjective sickness and inner-churning confusion as a piously noble contrition and admirable confession of his harmful deeds against the poor Africans as virtuous? I remember reading a textbook on biostatistics, which upheld that correlation is not causation. It is most likely he was overwhelmed with the often-felt post-trip despair and depression from the common feeling of ineffectiveness compared to the ideal "good" almost every missionary expected to accomplish. How do I know this? I have counseled and spent countless hours with numerous missionaries from the Western world, in attempts to help them sort through their internal post-trip self-criticisms and self-doubts. For some, even after participating in what were clearly meaningful and helpful mission experiences, they still expressed anxieties. They wondered about their responsibilities, if they ever made an impact, and how safely they carried themselves.

Had they worked hard enough to justify to their donors and supporters that their money for the short mission trip was not wasted? You ask most short-term and long-term missionaries about the cumbersome and anxiety-filled process of writing support updates from the so-called "mission field." Even though they claimed to "go for God," a preventative endeavor to make it clear that the trip wasn't about them, they still ask questions to make sure they are not making a mess by answering the call. Some wonder whether it was worth spending all that airfare to come all the way to do what the local people could do. People interested in missions are mostly preoccupied with the fears, shame, and false guilt of the looming possibility of not having a less-than-happy, spiritually appeasable, and heroic success story. Like Fikkert, they are afraid of presenting real failure and pain from an evangelical Christian culture that is hostile to receive mission lemons instead of lemonade. The Western missionary enterprise has long created romantic and triumphalist cultural deeds set on the pageantry homecoming narrative of its heroes from the dark and harrowing trenches of the "mission field."

The causes for Fikkert's reactions are also rooted in his fear of the newly unknown neighbor. From the start, he revealed the fears he experienced during his interactions with the poor people in a cross-cultural context in Uganda with Elizabeth, Grace, and the refugee community. Fikkert narrated his fear of and contempt for the "uncivilized" environment while visiting Grace's home in Uganda, crossing streams of mysterious "green slime" and seeing the poverty in which Grace lives. In fact, Fikkert's description is reminiscent of Joseph Conrad's Afro-pessimistic appetite and apocalyptic vision of Africa in his book *Heart of Darkness*. Fikkert narrates that he was "in the very bowels of hell" and wanted to get out of the slum community before dark.[4]

It seems to me that there is need for recourse in missions that redresses a missional vision under the grip of an empty social Darwinist[5] mechanism, which promotes the survival of the fittest and superior culture over the "cultural other."[6] The idea of sending "the best" to "the rest" is inconsistent with how Jesus calls his disciples to respond (Luke 10:27–28). But where do even well-intended missionaries acquire such a worldview? Betrand Russell, philosopher and educator who was awarded the Nobel Prize in literature, wrote, "Every man [or woman], wherever he [or she]

---

4. Fikkert and Corbett, *When Helping Hurts*, 24.

5. For a fuller discussion of social Darwinism and its impact on missions today, see MacLeod and Rehbock, *Darwin's Laboratory*, and Keim, *Mistaking Africa*.

6. Woodley, "Mission and the Cultural Other," 456.

goes, is encompassed by a cloud of comforting convictions, which move with [them] like flies on a summer day."[7] Whatever motivates such visceral reactions in global missions is an issue I'll discuss later in this chapter and others ahead. It is obvious that heightened fearfulness, mistrust, contempt, and signal anxiety fed suspicions and indifference, can lead to cynical and willful intentions and judgments that can negatively impact people who are interested in participating in missions from everywhere to anywhere. Elevated arousals of fear, false guilt, and anxiety in global missions will negatively infringe on a believer's participation and excitement about the invitation of Jesus for his disciples to be his witnesses to "Judea, Samaria, and the utmost of the world."[8] How has this call to participate with God the Father, God the Son, and God the Spirit been infiltrated by the unholy trinity of fear, anxiety, and false guilt? Isn't sharing the story of Jesus and the demonstration of God's love an invitation to die to self-centeredness and self-importance (Prov 3:34)?

Fear and anxiety that hurt you when helping

People are fallible creatures who live in a broken world and Christians are not the exception. In life in general, there are plenty of opportunities to be afraid at various levels in this world. This is why the Scriptures are littered with invitations and admonitions voicing the instruction of "do not be afraid." There are times when in certain instances fear, escorted by anxious feelings, can be deemed helpful in the presence of danger. In the book *The Gift of Fear,* Gavin De Becker discusses the upsides of instinct, asserting that when we do not listen to our instincts it can be costly in the end.[9] However, according to Joseph LeDoux, who is a neurological scientist, "Disorders of fear regulation are at the heart of psychopathologic conditions, including anxiety, panic, phobia."[10] LeDoux is referring to the crippling effects of fear, worry, terror, and trepidation. Consider, for example, some journalists' and political commentators' thoughts about electoral politics; especially during election periods around the world.

In this instance, the political fever in the United States in the 2016 presidential campaign is an appropriate bonanza of stirring the pot of fear

7. Russell, *Sceptical Essays,* 16.

8. Acts 1.

9. De Becker, *Gift Of Fear,* 21

10. LeDoux, "Emotion," 211.

as an intoxicating political weapon. The Southern Poverty Law Center observed that "the campaign is producing an alarming level of fear and anxiety."[11] That can't be a positive outcome. Fear and its equals have been part of the human experience since the beginning of time. Barry Glassner's book, *The Culture of Fear: Why Americans Are Afraid of the Wrong Things: Crime, Drugs, Minorities, Teen Moms, Killer Kids, Mutant Microbes, Plane Crashes, Road Rage, and So Much More,* provides more perspective. Glassner writes and explains how "some historical evidence also supports the hypothesis that people panic at the brink of centuries and millennia."[12] He further leads the reader to notice the historicity of

> "panic terror" in Europe around the year 1000 and the witch the hunts in Salem in the 1690s. As a complete or dependable explanation, though, the millennium hypothesis fails. Historians emphasize that panics of equal or greater intensity occur in odd years, as demonstrated by anti-Indian hysteria in the mid 1700s and McCarthyism in the 1950s. Scholars point out too that calendars cannot account for why certain fears occupy people at certain times (witches then, killer kids now).[13]

When you look back again in human history, it is clear that spiritually and physically debilitating phobias continue to ubiquitously pervade human life, affecting the presence of angst in human beings, which also influences some people's promotion of fear. In the twentieth century more people experienced war and conflict and were killed by the weapons of war in genocide and terrorism attacks than all of the other previous centuries before combined.

The National Geographic Visual Atlas of the World insists that the twentieth century is often described as the century of "total war," where modern weapon technological advancements have made people vulnerable and potential targets in warfare.[14] History is also littered with the tears of people whose experience of injustice and pain have caused them to seek freedom and exodus from injustice. Even the Israelites cried for food and God gave the manna (Exod 16). Elijah cried for God to stop the rain (1 Kgs 17:1; Jas 5:17–18). Joseph stored resources of grain to give to the community stricken with the famine (Gen 41). You can imagine the fear of hunger

11. Southern Poverty Law Center, "Trump Effect."
12. Glassner, *Culture of Fear,* xxviii.
13. Ibid., xx
14. *National Geographic Visual Atlas of the World,* 76.

and starvation driving their tears and petitions for help. It is no wonder that biblically defined fear, anxiety, and false guilt continue to be common threats to the idea of living the peaceful life that Jesus has given to believers around the world.

How does this unholy trinity interact with your daily life and have you felt and sensed its signals? I have. I have lived through war, lost relatives to HIV/AIDS at the height of the epidemic in Africa. My life has been spared from lethal illnesses to which I should have succumbed given the odds, but I am still here today. I have friends who have shared with me about the disheartening experiences they have encountered while living and working in emotionally rough conditions, where they witnessed orphans and refugees die from preventable issues, which are also directly related to lack of resources.

Global missions participants do face their own share of fears, anxiety, and guilt. For example, just ask anyone who has to fundraise for his or her mission trip about the levels of stress involved. Many even scramble for what to communicate, but usually default to sending out support letters. Which were lacking in regards to the representation of the shared biblical and ecclesial values of solidarity and oneness with believers and people in foreign cultural contexts (Rom 8:15–17).

Missionary fundraising and Christian humanitarianism have historically been set up to communicate fear through the portrayal of the missionized as stereotypically inferior. The system is set up to portray the people that God has called you to serve as less than you. The Filipino baby with flies on her lips, or the African child with a sad face and no shoes, is the sad story as to why they are going out and why the going-outer needs your money. As Beidelman observes in his book *Colonial Evangelism*, the language of missionary fundraising "from the West to the Rest" is dependent on propagating fear and panic of the situation of the dangerous unsaved savage, as opposed to the believers, in order to raise money for the missionary's needs and economic stability of the saving.[15] With the presence of worries, fear knocking on the doors of your heart, and the walls of division that might surround your life, it is noble to consider the Judeo-Christian perspective, which I believe is necessary to embrace in global missions. Gary R. Collins asserts,

> According to the Bible, there is nothing wrong with realistically acknowledging and trying to deal with the identifiable problems

15. Beidelman, *Colonial Evangelism*, xviii.

of life. To ignore danger is foolish and wrong. But it is also wrong, as well as unhealthy, to be immobilized by excessive worry. Such worry must be committed to prayer to God, who can release us from paralyzing fear or anxiety, and free us to deal realistically with the needs and welfare both of others and of ourselves.[16]

When it comes to global missions, I am deeply conflicted about the neglect and failure to counter the hyperconscious and destructive mind-set that scapegoats generosity and charity, while increasingly promoting negative stereotypes and conditioning fears that shape the believers' missionary journeys. Unless in the event that a person is narcissistically helping, which I know how easy it is to make bone-headed mistakes in missions, I still strongly maintain that helping people is not the problem. Most times it is the lack of information, wisdom, and failure to cultivate intercultural faithful friendship in missions.

Often, people who need help and are faced with abject poverty and stand the risk of not receiving the generous help they need of contextual information, mentorship and the ladder of opportunity, are the ones who face injustice. Why did they get into abject poverty and what keeps and holds people into abject poverty are necessary dialogical reflections to have. Is poverty the real problem to tackle? What about greed and wasteful habits? I think that any approach forward should include a both/and framework instead of an either/or strategy. Not all poverty is equal and not all poverty issues require a one-size-fits-all approach. Instead, the "when helping hurts" mind-set grossly and negatively lumps and labels the poor as victims of the so-called "culture of poverty."[17] It is a low level in missions when the Western missionary enterprise wildly wholesales such faulty views as a reason as to why people in Uganda face abject poverty. Would Jesus resort to such degraded categorical shaming and smearing of people and children faced with abject poverty? Not at all.

In fact, the spiritual act of service, of trying to help and love your neighbor, especially people who are genuinely in need and want your help both locally and globally in their process of personal growth, is a serious biblical mandate of love, life, and kindness. The Apostle John writes, "If anyone has material possessions and sees a brother or sister in need but has no pity on them, how can the love of God be in that person?"[18] The attitude

16. Collins, *Christian Counseling*, 66.

17. Fikkert and Corbett, *When Helping Hurts*, 187.

18. 1 John 3:17.

of indifference and holding back a believer's willingness to give when the opportunity to help the poor is urgently obvious and evident has become an epidemic issue within the evangelical Christian missiological circles. Greed and lack of generosity without strings attached is very hurtful. This has, in turn, encouraged fear, stinginess, anxiety, racial bias, power games, and false guilt in the guise of "stewardship" and restraint in being a "cheerful giver."[19] If you believe that God gave you the money, time, and other resources to meet your basic needs and more, then cheerfully help others. Give more than you limit yourself to give!

False guilt that hurts helping

When training and preparing missionaries and Christian humanitarian workers we must provide a correct and accurate narrative that the Bible provides about the gift of, and opportunity of participating in God's mission. We also must teach about the problem of false guilt. False guilt in missions is prevalent and Fikkert's experience is a perfect example. There are cases where people make clear mistakes, especially mistakes that are identified as harmful to the people impacted by the mistakes. In Fikkert's case, where he wrongly superimposed his American cultural meaning of "hurt" on the Uganda context, his was an illustration where false guilt got the better part of him. Is the meaning of harm and hurt the same in every culture? Or does Fikkert mean to dictate that his Western understanding of "hurt" is universal? I am mystified by how the author's self-professed experience in community development work could have failed to inquire and alter such notions.

In fact, I submit as a Ugandan that his bizarre missions proposal of not helping by giving money, but rather making the painfully broke refugees he met to foot the medicine bills of a poor, elderly, and sick recent convert to Christianity is a very low road; especially for the cost of a Starbucks coffee and a blueberry muffin. Why the aggression instead of being generous? He was led to a peculiar desire for innocence motivated by "False Evidence Appearing Real."[20] If you notice, that's FEAR spelled out and no missions strategy should ever be derived from fear. According to Hunt, "false guilt is based on self-condemning feelings that you have not lived up to your own expectations or those of someone else. False guilt arises when you blame

19. 2 Cor 9:6–7.

20. Steyn, *King Saul Spirit*, 197.

yourself even though you've committed no wrong."[21] The fear of people who do not look like you and do not worship like you is typically the fear of disapproval masked. Under the spell of false guilt, Western missionaries in Uganda and other foreign places imagine the worst possible conclusion. Yet in the host-culture reality, life's happenings are rarely as fatal and romantic as fear tends to dictate to missionaries like Fikkert.

God invites both the local and global church to generously participate in his mission in many ways; for example, giving of your time, finances, skills, talents, and other helpful resources. Dwelling on the pervasive advice of a negative and fearful mind-set, which serves to react to unsubstantiated worries, which in turn tends to freeze your will to serve and cause panic in a believer's attempt to venture into missions, will only feed into prejudice, insecurities, division, and rejection of people. Let me share with you a case in point where the negative stereotypic and supposedly cautionary advice about "helping that hurts," which plays in the fear of neighbor, absolutely derailed an opportunity for ministry in global missions. In this instance, not helping hurt just like the case of Mark, mentioned in chapter 1, who fell in a storm drain and died without help.

Dave and I first met in 2008 at the World AIDS Day event in Portland, Oregon. I was a guest speaker presenting on the HIV/AIDS epidemic response work myself and my friends in Uganda had been involved with. The prominently celebrated fight against HIV/AIDS was championed by the president and the first lady of Uganda. We visited together after the main presentation and immediately had a synergy of heart, mind-set, and camaraderie, having both moved to the United States from overseas and having a long history of giving and receiving global missionary endeavors. We remained sporadically in touch until the 2010 catastrophic earthquake in Haiti where an opportunity opened up for us to work together at the same Christian agency.

As the agency had raised several million dollars of public money for the Haiti response, we were told by one of the executive management staff that we had a "clean slate" to develop partnership opportunities for the well-being of people as part of a new strategic department to develop healthy partnerships with churches. In March 2010 we headed for Haiti together to explore opportunities alongside the newly established Haiti office delivering emergency response.

---

21. Hunt, *Guilt*, 14.

Through the process of networking we met several Haitian pastors, and focused on listening and learning from our Haitian colleagues. We met a wonderful man called Pastor Jean Baptiste (his real name has been changed). In the aftermath of the earthquake the community had given unto his care many children who had lost their parents. Pastor Jean Baptiste and his wife were also caring for children whose homes were destroyed and the parents were living in tent camps too unsafe for children. In his home they were caring for over forty children. The day we first arrived we were greeted at the doorway by all the children singing songs of welcome and songs to Jesus as we rejoiced together in the goodness of God. Singing together was so refreshing, indeed a clear reminder that it's God our maker "who gives songs in the night."[22]

The earthquake in Haiti had changed the landscape of the community in an instant. Pastor Jean and his wife, who were busy seeking the well-being of these children, embraced the tasks at hand. They were in the thick of it. As leaders of a small Haitian nonprofit, a culturally contextual mechanism was already in place on how Pastor Jean and his wife planned on feeding and comforting the parentless and homeless children. The community entrusted the livelihood and well-being of children in their care. All that was needed was friendship and financial investments to help the children. According to the pastor, his wife, and other church elders, a grant of $50,000 to the pastor's organization could purchase land on the outskirts of the city in order to develop a new home and resource center for the wider community affected by the massive earthquake. Their plan was to move the children from their overcrowded home to a new community center to begin a new future for the local community, with an immediate home for those orphaned. There would be a school for the children of the neighboring families, with vegetable gardens and small animal husbandry.

Yes, some assets were present in the form of everything that everyone was trying to do to help: their time, their days that they went without sleep as they received children, their energy as they pulled out bodies, and the little money they had. Every molecule within their very being was already at work. But they still needed money given with no strings attached. The notion that assets already exist should never be used as a reason for not helping. That's like looking at a man struggling with one leg and saying, "lets wait until his other leg falls off before we help."

22. Job 35:10.

As we left Haiti to head back to the headquarter offices, we were excited and thankful to God for this newfound friendship. Dave completed the project proposal and then we met with the leadership of the organization to share such a wonderful opportunity. Reality hit us hard. The authorities at headquarters in the United States told us this was not a viable project because this was not what the organization does. The organization that prided itself on working with and helping "the indigenous people" raised its hand against them. We were asked, "How can we trust Pastor Jean when we don't know him?" "This is not what we do. We don't build buildings, we are a health and medical focused organization"; "This is not our core competency"; "This is not a sustainable project"; "We will be on the hook for more money after this initial transfer." Conditioned fear and assumptions resounded and hissed with all sorts of excuses. It was fascinating. Pastor Jean and his work were dismissed on distrust.

We were asking for a grant of $50,000 from a pot of $5,000,000 that had been raised from the public in direct response to the earthquake. Myself, Pastor Jean, and Dave had spent numerous hours together using our experience and education to network and develop friendships, and we prayed together in belief that God had led us to this opportunity. We wanted to be generous and invest in building faithful friends and interdependent partnerships. However, it was surprising to witness the amount of contempt with which Pastor Jean and his community were treated. How was investing in these little precious lives and providing safe homes, education, access to food, and community life not going to increase the physical and mental health of this community? How was accompanying and being accomplices with the Haitian pastor, his wife, and his church in their God-given vision providing help that hurts?

Organizational leadership on no real basis found the Haitian pastor suspicious, guilty before proven, and not trustworthy. Was the pastor guilty of being a stereotyped identity who was caught up in the wake of a devastating earthquake? Were we staring at the problem of the "blame the Haitian" game? Dr. Paul Farmer, professor of global health at Harvard University, writes about "the image Haitians found waiting for them when, in 1970, many emigrated to United States: 'Haitians were portrayed as ragged, wretched and pathetic and were said to be illiterate, superstitious, disease-ridden and backward peasants."[23]

23. Farmer, *AIDS and Accusation*, 4.

It is possible that such aggressive preconceived beliefs and lingering attitudes might have played a part in the hardness of heart demonstrated by the leaders of a missions relief organization's refusal to help out in the scenario of the Haitian Christian family who led a small national nonprofit organization and were trying to responsibly help children and families affected by disaster. How about the organization itself? Did it have "best practices" and thus live up to the standards of judgment with which it held Pastor Jean, his wife, and their Haitian community? Not at all. To begin with, the organization's methodologies for giving were self-preserving. We watched as the organization spent over $100,000 on the lease and renovation of another building to house its medical teams of doctors going to a certain city in Haiti. After six months, the building was no longer needed because the initial disaster response phase was over. Dave, the Haitian staff, and I stood on the roof of that house wondering if we could lease this out to someone else in order to recover some of the renovation cost, ultimately to no avail. Was that sustainable?

I strongly believe that Pastor Jean should have been given the $50,000 grant as an extended hand of faithful friendship and interdependent partnerships without any strings attached. As Luke writes about one of the profound beatitudes, "It is more blessed to give than receive."[24] This is helping that works. Together with Pastor Jean, his family, and community, we should have worked hard to raise more money for continued help alongside the local long-term initiatives of providing quality education, and we should have encouraged their passion for farming vegetables, goats, and other necessary investments that would support the vision over the long haul. We should have committed to respectfully and truthfully telling their story to others, and worked hand-in-hand over a sustained period of time.

The Christian relief agency had plenty of money but abdicated its role to help this much-deserving community heavily impacted by the 7.0 earthquake. Giving would have worked in this case and would have been in direct orthodoxy to the Scriptures. Paul makes it clear to the Christian communities involved in global mission in the New Testament that those with more resources than people undergoing hardship should "supply what they need."[25] The phobia of Pastor Jean as the damaged cultural other furthers the stigmatization of his identity as a person deemed to lack the technocratic skills and "voice" preferred by the Western Christian NGO. Such

24. Acts 20:35.
25. 2 Cor 8:12b–15.

an attitude contributed more confusion in the presence of despair. Pastor Jean was confused and so were we. The organization claimed to be giving voice to the voiceless, but they delivered hopelessness by withholding the help and resources Pastor Jean needed. In this occasion, who created the "voiceless"? Through apathy, the Western Christian organization also disrespected and dismissed the Haitian pastor's voice and in effect muted it to create the "voiceless."

The historical mines in the mission field

Most mission groups are motivated by the biblical commission to proclaim the gospel and work on humanitarian and social justice causes. However, in the case of global missions, Christian groups from completely different cultural contexts, for instance Christian groups from Uganda and the United States, face intercultural challenges—a major and common hurdle, but one that's frequently ignored in both local and global missions from which groups experience relational pain, fear, anxiety, and false guilt as a stigma and as the reality of social identity. For instance, Goffman articulates the fact that negative attitudes based on social identity stigma tend to target the differences in people.[26] Such effects are common ways to discredit the relationship attempts between Western and non-Western missionaries.

Such attitudes are of old. The Old Testament writer narrates a story in which Moses, who was God's lead mouth piece to Pharaoh about the emancipation of the Jews from slavery, came face to face with the negative ethnocentric barriers contingent on Zipporah's (Moses' wife) social identity as an African woman. In fact, God's response to Miriam's (Moses' sister) derogatory treatment of Zipporah was not pleasant. Check out God's verdict and disapproval on Miriam's bigoted rejection of her brother Moses' marriage to Zipporah (Num 12:10).

In the New Testament, Peter, who was one of Jesus' apostles, was instructed by God while in a trance to face his ongoing prejudice and the distinctions between Jew and Gentile (Acts 10). James instructs believers to be careful and avoid favoritism (Jas 2), which also propagates negative stereotypes of one party in unjustified favor of another. James's exhortation is pertinent in global missions since along with some of the positive impacts of the eighteenth and nineteenth century missionary enterprise, namely building hospitals and supporting education, there was also the

---

26. Goffman, *Stigma*, 3.

expansion of imperialism, which was rampantly predicated on the no-tion of the superior reaching and taming the inferior. As Amy Stambach recounts in her book *Faith in Schools: Religion, Education and American Evangelicals in East Africa*, "First European colonists, then the World Bank, and now American missionaries, their argument went, treated Africans as childlike and incapable of self-governance."[27] While such attitudes might have mellowed out, the "illusion of superiority"[28] that's plagued the West-ern Christian missionary enterprise still poses a challenge.

This is why it is necessary for modern Western short-term, long-term missionaries and Western missiological technocrats, surrounded as they are on every hand with evidence of their economic and social ascendancy, need to be alert.[29] Why? They must learn to die to self as Jesus instructed, by en-gaging in the fight of the temptation of the "secret" feelings of superiority, as these attitudes result in the setbacks that emerge from the "great [missionary] complex" over some of the people who can hardly subsist.[30]

In fact, to illustrate further, a former US missionary to Uganda of Cau-casian descent recently told me that since he returned, he has been motivat-ing fellow believers to not take for granted that he can get a lot done for Jesus Christ because of his skin color. What a destructive mentality to the idea of a credible Christian witness. It is the US missionary's right to talk about his complexion, but not in a manner that promotes race baiting in global missions. Besides, does the US missionary assume that all Ugandans wor-shipfully adore his skin color as Caucasian? Does he also mean to embrace the entire negative colonial legacies that many people associate with Western imperialism, which in many instances accompanied Christendom?

According to Acemoglu and Robinson, such association historically dates back to the Spanish expansion and colonization of the Americas in 1519, where the indigenous peoples had to give tribute and labor services, in exchange for which the *encomendero* was charged with converting them to Christianity.[31] How is it that the American missionary thinks race-based missions are viable? Whatever happened to sharing the gospel? The Apostle Paul valued the rights afforded him, but he decried cruel manipulation of any rights when he writes, "We have not made use of this right, but we endure

---

27. Stambach, *Faith in Schools*, 3.

28. Bonk, *Missions and Money*, 50.

29. Ibid., 51.

30. Ibid.

31. Acemoglu and Robinson, *Why Nations Fail*, 13.

anything rather than put an obstacle in the way of the Gospel of Christ."[32] When did God's mission be about erecting dividing walls (Eph 2)? This kind of egocentric and ethnocentric arrogance is harmful to the helping and hospitality ministry in missions. Race baiting in missions does not work and you would be hard pressed to find any biblical evidence in support of such desperate and exploitative tactics. It is a major injury to followers of Jesus Christ in the Western world as well as to those in the majority world. Such bait-and-switch, us-verses-them strategies obstruct rather than encourage healthy mission strategies of mutuality, unity, and reciprocity.

The historical European project of colonialism and Western imperialism enjoyed the use of power enforced with their guns, but Christ's ambassadors should be equipped with love, empathy, and kindness. But in today's globalizing world, transnationalists travel for all sorts of reasons and most of them are armed with briefcases. What has changed? As I travel through the numerous airports I've been fortunate to experience, I've watched a number of people traversing through as they check in at the ticket counters, kiosks, and the Internet cafés. I figuratively wonder what agendas and stereotypes people carry in their briefcases and cultural backpacks.

The global church in its intercultural, missiological presence on the other hand is called to unity, faithful friendship, and a gospel-centric mindfulness in global missions practices (1 Cor 12:12). In order for healthy intercultural friendship to flourish, there is need to reshape and prepare believers to be mindful of the relational implications and the menaces of a fear-based, anxiety- and panic-driven mind-set. Elmer explains that during a workshop for about sixty North American mission executives where the theme was "education for missionaries," the number one issue was, without question, that the greatest problem in missions is relational breakdowns.[33] It is necessary to add that the consideration of situational dynamics in which relationships are strangled matter immensely. People and their friendship networks are inextricably intertwined with their sociocultural situations. Yet with the popularity of the "helping hurts" mentality, as promoted by Fikkert, many fail to question the negative and deep assumption that belay such a mind-set and its negative impact on societies like Uganda. How is it that once again that it's Fikkert and Corbett from "the West" who prescribe what's best for Ugandans and Africans, while omitting the inspiring stories of what many Ugandans are already doing for themselves? Theirs is a mind-set that stokes prejudice,

---

32. 1 Cor 9.

33. Elmer, *Cross-Cultural Conflict,* 33.

apathy, an anti-giving and anti-generosity environment based on fear and panic, and puts the Christian mission and its witness in jeopardy. This is not helpful to the global church. This is truly harmful.

Blame and self-afflicted hurt in missions

I feel frustrated, along with others, with the key story that frames Fikkert's book. The story is the centerpiece of his book and is prevalent in the greater mind-set. There is a seismic problem that is a runaway train that encourages a dysfunctional approach to humanity, giving and helping relationships. Categorically, Fikkert sees it fit to refer to himself as "the 'mzungu'[34] who . . . felt sick . . . about the enormous amount of harm to the church, its pastor, and to the refugees . . . and to Grace herself"[35] caused by giving Grace $8 for her medicine. He gave this out of his own pocket instead of what he believed he should have done by corralling "small amounts" of money from the poor refugees. I do not fault Fikkert for feeling sick; however, as a Ugandan who is also familiar with both the Ugandan and the US cultural context, I do not recognize the harm that he claims to have committed. In my view, his mistakes are three-fold. One, he cites the wrong problems. Two, he writes the wrong story for his book. Helping Grace with $8 is *not* the problem and helping in and of itself never hurts. Three, he misconstrued and exploited the accidental fact of his skin complexion or what his skin tone presents. The term "Mzungu" is a hangover from days of colonialism where the superior dictated life for the inferior, and unfortunately today many from the West still play into it. There is no need for racial insensitivity to be injected into the work of the gospel, and it is especially curious when coming from the racial cauldron of America. It does not build into our unity, both for Americans and Ugandans.

What exactly was going on here? It is fear, anxiety, and false guilt that propel Fikkert's grief over the $8, which he claims caused danger to the Africans he met and the error in buying an elderly sick woman in Uganda the medicines she needed.

34. The term "muzungu" is used to describe American missionaries and Western expatriates. Bizimana explains that muzungu (plural: bazungu) traditionally refers to white people of European and North American decent. In the course of time, the definition of this word was expanded to include all light-skinned people, even those fair-skinned people of non-white ancestry. Muzungu also carries connotations of wealth, since the main characteristic of the colonial masters was affluence.

35. Fikkert and Corbett, *When Helping Hurts*, 26.

In the case of Fikkert's felt sickness, the metaphorical "virus" that made him sick, he did not catch it in Uganda.

In this scenario, a US missionary tried to force an imaginary Western subcultural and ideological fix to the problem of resource poverty evident in the lack of medicine (a resource) for an ill woman in the Ugandan context. He assumes the role of a super moral patron and Western expatriate with trusteeship over the "cultural other." He is helplessly unable to be receptive to an opportunity given him by God, in the presence of "the poor," to help through a vulnerable, empathy-based and joyfully generous posture.

For anyone who isn't clear about the vexing nature of such methods, perhaps the words of the first Indian bishop of the Anglican Church in India, given to delegates at the 1910 Edinburgh Conference, might serve an illuminative purpose. Bishop V. S. Azariah lamented that missionaries, except for a few of the very best, seem to fail very largely in getting rid of an air of patronage and condescension, and in establishing a genuinely brotherly and sisterly friendship among equals. He continued to acknowledge that missionaries have given their goods to feed the poor. They have given their lives in some cases. However, as a reverberation of the apostle Paul, the Indian bishop calls for faithful and loving friendship when he says, "Give us friends."

Fikkert was hamstrung by his phobia of foreigners, potential friends who are interested in faithful friendship and interdependent partnerships in their cultural context. It is probable that Fikkert's condescending attitudes toward "the poor" or the cultural other in Uganda are the real problems to be fixed. On the contrary to Fikkert's flawed story is a similar situation, which I've already narrated, in the opening chapter. In this particular instance, Dave acted positively in his interaction with the sick lady in Fang, Thailand, in an intercultural context without a historical narrative plagued by a historicity of colonial prejudice between his British background and that of the elderly Thai lady.

I am also deeply perplexed as to what *When Helping Hurts'* seeks to endorse. Are the authors endorsing a self-inflicted and depreciatory guilt that leads Fikkert to feel bad about giving his hard-earned dollars to lazy, and inconsiderate African refugees? Do they mean to show that poor people in places like Uganda do not have the intellectual ability to think about the "best ways" to help one another; until Fikkert arrives on the scene? Must it take the "exclusively . . . masterful leadership of the" muzungu (as former

US President Theodore Roosevelt put it while on a hunting escapade in Africa)[36] to awaken their dangerously asleep minds in the slum of Uganda?

Yet still, the wrong assumptions that Fikkert, the Presbyterian economist of Dutch descent, champions regarding the nature of the reality of resource poverty in places like Uganda persist. I address more of the misunderstanding of poverty issue in the following chapters. It is bemusing how Fikkert could witness an elderly woman in need of medicine, provide the medicine, and then feel sick about being kind and generous. Wow! Am I the only who is surprised and dismayed by this idea of "when helping hurts"? What would you do? If your Auntie is sick and needs medicine, and she has a prescription to buy the medicine but does not have the money, would you buy her the medicine, especially when you have the money and she doesn't? Or would you instead feel sick about helping her, all the while wishing that the opportunity for Christian love responsibility fell on her neighbor? Why is Grace different from your Auntie? What barriers were present in the missionary endeavor between Grace of Uganda and the US Presbyterian economist of Dutch descent? A prejudicial wall?

In this story, Fikkert's $8 is far less to him, proportionally, than the small amounts of discretionary money he assumes the members of the refugee community have. Fikkert is the wealthiest man in that slum community, and all of the members know that; they see the clothes, the hotel where he is staying, the food he can eat, his education status, and the fact that he comes from a wealthy economy. What would you expect from an expatriate from the United States who has the money to spend on a six-month sabbatical with his entire family in Uganda? Besides, in African culture by and large, the most appropriate and loving response is always hospitality and generosity that includes the exchange of gifts and resources. The reality of not being a mindful giver from a position of such wealth contributes to people's levels of suffering and is a form of rejection of the very same people that God is calling you to love. Relational rejection hurts and is painful.

My desire to come to the United States was in part to continue the journey of learning about my fellow brothers and sisters who came to Uganda on both short-term and long-term missions. They helped out in many ways, yet there was so much relational friction and pain for all involved. I have spent countless hours discussing and analyzing why so much pain and rejection is caused in the arena and endeavors of global missions.

36. Roosevelt, *African Game Trails*, 9.

The major problem of Fikkert and the mind-set he promotes is one where he encounters stereotype threats in his missiological interactions.

We will discuss in depth the profundity of this well-researched phenomenon in the following chapters. There is nothing uplifting in encouraging Christians to develop mission strategies that blame the pathologies of poverty onto the very poor themselves while esteeming a Christian's decision to withhold the biblical mandate to give resources with no strings attached. Helping is not the problem. In fact, helping your neighbor and especially people who need and want your help both locally and globally is a serious biblical and holistic mandate of love. The Apostle John writes, "If anyone has material possessions and sees a brother or sister in need but has no pity on them, how can the love of God be in that person?"[37] This phenomenon of not giving when the opportunity to help the poor is urgently obvious and evident, has become an endemic issue within the evangelical Christian missiological and charitable infrastructure. Giving has become so conditional and systematized that the rules and regulations have fostered fear, stinginess, and anxiety under the guise of "stewardship" and restraint in being a "cheerful giver."[38]

Unfortunately, so many ministry projects are delivered from the "best in the West to the Rest" through a prescriptive approach, like a set menu at a restaurant for a meal to be given to the host community whether they like it or want it or not. Incidentally, this kind of approach pits Fikkert against the people he actually needs to work with in mutual partnership. In post-colonialism studies, Fikkert and some humanitarian partners propped up by economic and class power are the patrons who believe that they are needed—that they are the superior ones who will the fix the inferior society, because the inferior society is made up of inferior people who are responsible for the pathologies that affect their community. The patron has come to whip everyone into shape because the poverty they face, be it resource issues or a perceived spiritual "need," are issues perceived as innate to their ethnicity and their kind of humanity. Fikkert and the humanitarian also capitalize on the human labor of the poor, as it is typically the superior who makes the most money from the endeavors and experiences. Is this the exploitation of the resource poor in favor of the resource rich? The lack of practicing genuine help is often accompanied by wastefulness. Further,

37. 1 John 3:17.

38. 2 Cor 9:6–7.

pain is inflicted when local people see the abundance of resources wasted in the custodianship of the church.

The Ugandans, and the Haitians whose stories I have mentioned in earlier sections, are all in the same boat—a different boat than Fikkert and Corbett and the Christian relief agencies. You want to be on the boat that is not sailing on the mission waters of fearfulness, anxiety, and false guilt, but on the boat where Jesus was with the disciples, where he took care of his disciples, where he loved them abundantly amid their fears and treated them with generosity. He performed miracles, which calmed the turbulent sea, and in capturing their attention, Jesus calmed the disciples' nerves of anxiety. We want to be on the boat where perfect love casts out fear, sailing on the waters of fearlessness with Jesus as the captain of the ship of God's local and global mission.

Help locally, build faithful friendships/partnerships globally

In summary

The insistence on missions guided by fear, anxiety, and false guilt is an injustice. In his "Letter from Birmingham Jail" written on April 16, 1963, Dr. Martin Luther King, Jr. wrote, "Injustice anywhere is a threat to justice everywhere."[39] The stigmatization of helping the poor is an unjust reaction in current Christian missions and we must look at where the source of this spiritual ebola comes from. The greater mind-set's response to withholding giving based on fear, anxiety, and control is an abdication from biblical justice. It is the promotion of injustice in place of administering faithful friendship that takes care of the poor as an expression of the gospel both locally and globally. Micah, the Old Testament prophet, asked on behalf of Israel, "With what shall I come before the Lord?" (Mic 6:6).

God doesn't answer with advice to his followers to focus their help and financial support in their local community only and not globally. For that is gross localism. Rather, God invited believers to be and do three things: "To do justice, and to love kindness, and walk humbly with your God" (Mic 6:8). Many Christians from Europe and the United States are involved with ministries in Uganda and around the world that are established to help orphans, end poverty, train pastors, "save" and rehabilitate former child soldiers, etc. However, the non-Western missionary presence has always

39. King, "Letter from Birmingham Jail," 2.

been in existence as well. For example, in Uganda, Ugandans propagated the gospel. According to Hastening,

> Buganda is the only place in Africa where there was both large-scale conversions to Christianity in the pre-colonial era and a mass conversion movement within the early colonial age. The latter was most certainly dependent upon the former, and while the arrival of British rule in the early 1890s facilitated it, the explanation for what happened is to be found less in any colonial logic than in the initial conversions and stormy events of the 1880s, leading up to the political and military triumph of the Christian minority in a situation when British rule was certainly not anticipated, at least upon the African side.[40]

The above demonstration of non-Western involvement in the spread of Christianity is part of a storytelling renaissance, rooted in the valida-tion of Ugandan Christians' role in missions. It is a testament to the fact that God is always at work in people's communities and that God precedes all human efforts. God is there before the missionary arrives. This should encourage missionaries from everywhere to anywhere to try to find one another and form faithful friendship and interdependent partnerships in the gospel instead of going it alone. We have so much to learn from one another if we can look at each other through the eyes of respect and dignity.

To further illustrate, let me introduce you to a favorite phrase: "Cook-ing the meal together." But if you attempt to use it, please be mindful of sloganeering over the slow and demanding work of faithful friendship building, which is illustrated in the solutions I submit in chapter 6. Believ-ers seeking to serve in missions both locally and globally need to resist the temptation of what Duane Elmer, author of *Cross-Cultural Conflict: Building Relationships for Effective Ministry*, calls "the win-lose strategy."[41] The hunger for control over gospel partners in global missions is bankrupt when it comes to "cooking the friendship meal together," of building a com-mon voice. What was Fikkert's sin and wrongdoing that generated the guilt he laments of while doing missions in Uganda? Guilt tends to arise when behaviors and actions clearly break laws and rules against fellow human beings and God. As Becker puts it:

> Guilt feelings arise from actions, which break down our relation-ships, especially those vitalizing relationships with mother and

40. Hastings, *Church in Africa*, 464.
41. Elmer, *Cross-Cultural Conflict*, 34.

father, then siblings, and later schoolmates. For an adult, these are relationships with family, spouse, peers, colleagues, and members of the community.[42]

False guilt also presents itself in moments of anxiety and fear based on hypothetical ideas. For example, Fikkert claims to have failed due to not considering "local assets that already existed in this slum, assets that included small amounts of money."[43] You can almost see Fikkert overthinking and panicking about the possibility in the manner of "what if they have the money to help but . . . " He must not know the pain and misery of abject poverty. The sense of false guilt and the "sickness" from which Fikkert derived the title of his and Corbett's book does not ring true of a person with empathy and compassion; instead, it further conforms what the notable Lakota Chief Luther Standing Bear observed as "troubled with primitive fears."[44] It is difficult to perceive how equitable proposals can emerge out of Fikkert's negative stereotypical missional strategies that are mostly affirmative of self-fulfilling negative stereotypes about majority world Christian and Western missionaries. Isn't there a better way out? A biblical message that calls Western evangelical missionaries "to act justly and to love mercy and to walk humbly with your God."[45]

Christians from everywhere and anywhere need each other, but the spirit of fear, laden with indifference and greedy attitudes of localism, are stocking missions with the wages of rejection. Some people, who should spend time investing in the hard work of friendships and therefore experience the transference of resource, seem to find a weird sense of comfort in becoming the eye that says to the hand, "I don't need you!"(1 Cor 12:21). I was once asked by a pastor of global missions in a church in Portland, Oregon, as to whether a believer in the West and a believer from a non-Western context need each other. What an inquiry! If Christians harbor the suspicion that unity among the global church Christians might not be necessary, then how are Christians from various intercultural background supposed to work together? Was the pastor aware that the scriptural response is a resounding and emphatic, "Yes we do need one another!" The

42. Becker, *Guilt*, 16.

43. Fikkert and Corbett, *When Helping Hurts*, 130.

44. Takaki, *Different Mirror*, 10.

45. Mic 6:8.

Apostle Peter writes, "All of you must live in harmony, be understanding, love as brothers, and be compassionate and humble."[46]

More so, without unity and seeking partnership in the gospel, believers render themselves liable to communicating rejection, which renders the church's opportunity to share Christ's love into the demonstration of "the pain of being excluded."[47]

It is important to realize that the mind-set that is promoted by Fikkert is not universal and that there are other intercultural voices that provide a biblical formational approach to giving, which is what this book seeks to champion.

In his book The Hole in Our Gospel, Stearns narrates how values of kindness towards people in need of resources both at the macro and individual level can be of demonstrable impact. Stearns captures a moment of when helping works. In a meeting arranged between Octaviana and her three children, who live in a mountain community high in the Andes, and Stearns from Seattle, Washington, in the United States, there was an impressive display of generosity. The story maintains that Octaviana's husband had just died from respiratory problems, leaving her and her children alone to fend for themselves in the harsh rural mountain environment. As Stearns became aware of Octaviana's situation and confronted his own abundant ability to help, Stearns notes, "I will return to my comfortable home in a few days. I'll tuck my children into their comfortable beds and then read them a story. The familiar routines of my life will resume again."[48] Stearns promised Octaviana and her children that upon returning back to the United States, he "would not forget her."[49] Instead of wishing for the local community to muster a few cents for the widow and her children, Stearns and World Vision helped. They responded to the need at hand, gave money directly, and demonstrated biblical love and hope in the situation. No one was hurt; it was the right action and a proper demonstration of helping that works.

46. 1 Pet 3:8.
47. Weir, "Pain of Social Rejection," 50.
48. Stearns, Hole in Our Gospel, 169.
49. Ibid.

Chapter 3

Something's In the Air

Not everything that is faced can be changed. But nothing can be changed until it is faced.

JAMES BALDWIN

Being ignorant is not so much a shame, as being unwilling to learn.

BENJAMIN FRANKLIN

YOUR DESIRE AND WILLFUL act to help others is a good thing. Yet, what you do not know about being fearful and chronically anxious will set you back. I want to introduce you to a global perspective about stereotype threat in intercultural missions. According to Dr. Claude M. Steele and Joshua Aronson, stereotype threat is being at risk of confirming, as self-charac-teristic, a negative stereotype about one's group. What Steele has termed "something in the air."[1]

That "something in the air," in other words, is a self-fulfilling prophecy of the life predicament of stereotype threat that we find front and center in Fikkert's missions experience in Uganda and its impact on our daily lives is more than we know.

Unfortunately, such a significant fact escaped Fikkert and Corbett in their good intentions of trying to advise the Western evangelical commu-nity on global missions. This advice has been amplified within the greater mind-set of intercultural missions. Yet stereotype threat should have been a strong focus since it's the prevalent metaphorical intercultural banana peel

1. Steele, "Threat in the Air," 613–29.

over which the missionaries trip up constantly in our discourse. Case in point, in my view as a Ugandan Christian, Fikkert can't quite seem to point his finger at the irritating stubbornness underneath his skin from the word "muzungu" in order to scratch where it really itches. So much so that the term muzungu is crowned on the throne in the front seat of the introduction of their book. After you find out the meaning of the term, I believe you will also wonder as to why the American missionary of Caucasian descent thought it necessary to magnify that aspect of his social standing and ethnicity. What is his predicament? Anyone is entitled to write about what he or she believes might be worthwhile. However, in certain instances like in the case of satire and sarcasm genres, would it go over well if a missionary from Africa made his "blackness" a negative cautionary disadvantage or else a strategic advantage in the helping missions ministry? But just what does the intercultural word muzungu mean? What is its history? Is it a term that propagates and plays fast and loose within a rapidly globalizing world? You might not be aware of it, but stereotype threat and its influence on social identities, like that of muzungu, have played significant roles in intercultural relational dynamics in the global church. Bizimana explains that muzungu (plural: bazungu) literally means "somebody who supersedes somebody else." The phrase traditionally refers to white people of European and North American decent.

In the course of time, the definition of this word was expanded to include all light-skinned people, even those fair-skinned people of non-white ancestry. For example, the term can also include other ethnic groups in the West, namely, Latinos, Africa-Americans, Asian-Americans, and all European ethnicities. This reminds me of when I was working in Uganda with numerous groups from the United States. I saw first-hand the distress, dismay, and painful confusion when African-Americans in particular were greeted, treated, and called the m-word. They were hit with what I have come to understand as a rather universal melancholic "newcomer effect." It is a nondiscriminatory effect in global missions, which even infiltrates the processes of assimilation and adaptation even though it is at times helpful in intercultural intelligence. The melancholic side of being a foreign newcomer unveils a rude awakening which both hits the new incoming missionary and interplays with the host culture alike, to the extent that people begin "to see a new map of the world, one that was frightening in its simplicity, suffocating in its implications."[2]

2. Obama, *Dreams From My Father*, 85.

The feelings of fear and anxiety for any newcomer in a missional, intercultural situation are indicative of how stereotype threats operate. In effect, to grapple with the forces of stereotypes in global missions, you should seek to understand the larger forces that shaped Christian global missions. The term "muzungu" also carries connotations of wealth, since the main characteristic of the colonial masters was affluence, control, and power.[3] Other stereotypes associated with North American Christians from the surveys completed by Ugandans include "law abiding,"[4] "rich, confidant, intelligent, enterprising, military experts, happy . . . [and] liberal."[5] Ugandan participants also noted that certain American short-term missionaries "do not know world geography."[6] It has been shaped by the ubiquitous and conspicuous history of colonialism and imperialism on the Africa continent. According to Schipper, "all over the world, people have sought explanation for the mysteries of the environment around them. To the people of Africa, the rule of the white man was one of the those mysteries."[7] This is why I am passionately and fully persuaded that this book will provide you with a much-needed global perspective on some of the key areas that so easily avoid the global church's relationships.

Perception, impact, and representation in global missions

A biblically grounded intercultural perspective can help missionaries from anywhere and everywhere appreciate the complex influence of perception and the need for the removal of cultural blinders. One may object, saying, "Isn't this too complicated when we are just supposed to be witnesses of the proclamation of the gospel?" Indeed, for a follower of Jesus Christ, the messaging of the gospel is primary; however, how you are perceived in your missional work is equally primary and matters in intercultural contexts. For example, a new missionary called John felt so strongly about the obligation to share his faith. One day, when his neighbor returned from work, John walked up to him and started sharing his faith. The neighbor asked John if he could get home first, and invited John to perhaps visit on another day. John insisted and even told his neighbor of how he pitied him for rejecting

3. Bizimana, *White Paradise*, 21.

4. Peace Apiyo, interview by the author, June 6, 2014, Kampala, Uganda.

5. John Muhumuza, interview by the author, January 14, 2014, Kampala, Uganda.

6. Peace Apiyo, interview by the author, June 6, 2014, Kampala, Uganda.

7. Schipper, *Imagining Insiders*, 31.

a chance to listen to his message. You can guess as to whether they ever met again. John is entitled to the desire to share about his faith, but in this situation John appeared desperate and disrespectful. The scripture's advice to John about such an interaction is, "Do it with gentleness and respect,"[8] or as Eugene Peterson puts it, "Always with the utmost courtesy." John thought he was right in his role as a representative, but he turned out to be terribly off base, that led to a poor perception. He represented an anxious presence and an identity not of the gospel but of a representative of basic human impulses that made his neighbor atwitter.

Back to the example of Fikkert and the lopsided impact of his intentions in the attempt to warn the Western church about how they ought to treat people in Uganda and the majority world. His is an appropriate demonstration of a Western missionary in the twenty-first century encumbered with an anxious presence about his social identity and neighbor. On the contrary, Edwin Friedman in his book, *A Failure of Nerve: Leadership in the Age of the Quick Fix*, advocates for a self differentiated "non-anxious presence."[9] Known or unknown to Fikkert, he is still affected by the vestiges of stereotype threat that were bolstered by the negative transformation ushered in by Western imperialism in global missions.

While in Uganda, Fikkert seems preoccupied with the anxiety, fear, and a mental appraisal of a self that is dependent on how Ugandans perceive "white people."[10] He is not sure how they perceive him. Is he accepted or rejected? Were the onward lookers admiring or making fun of him? The anxious, fearful presence he projects is about the very experience of identity differences in missions. Fikkert is caught between the rock of perception and the hard place of representation. Such an experience is common because of basic human impulses, which are attached to fears of a negative stereotype contingent on his identity that proclaims to be at play. John, like Fikkert, fears that stereotype threat will invalidate their "good intentions," innocence, and professional and technocratic experience.

Like Fikkert, many people experience stereotype threat in missions several times because of the negative stereotypes that exist about one or more of their personal, cultural, or racial attributes. You witness the negative impact of stereotype threat when its targets cave into moments of introspection as to whether they are being judged or not. When on the receiving

8. 1 Pet 3:15.
9. Friedman, *Failure of Nerve*, 183.
10. Fikkert and Corbett, *When Helping Hurts*, 23.

side of stereotype threat in missions, you have tensions about whether you could be judged, but you still don't know for sure whether you are in or out. This is important to notice because such a prospect can infringe on and distract a missionary's intercultural attentiveness in negative ways that curtail one's missional performance. A timely example is evident in Fikkert's moment of distress. He writes, "Finally, there was me, the mzungu, and all which that word represents: money, power, money, education . . . superiority."[11] Interestingly, Fikkert appears to have considered what it means to possess the "white people" social identity in intercultural and global missions. Could it be that while in Uganda, Fikkert encountered a threat on his social identity in a way far and beyond a "just normal" routine? More revealing is his regret of helping an elderly and terminally ill woman in Uganda, and his delusional plot of dissociation, disengagement, and self-preservation, and his preference to be a bystander, like the priest in the story of the Good Samaritan.

It is revealing when close attention is given to the effects of ignoring, underestimating, and even not knowing the cost of operating out of anxiety and fear in missions. I will further demonstrate to you the impact of fears and anxieties in reference to "identities contingences"[12] in global missions. Identity contingences, are the things you have to deal with in a situation because you have a given social identity, because you are poor, old, white, black, male, Asian, female, or short- or long-term missionary.[13] I am grateful for the numerous opportunities I've had to work extensively with missionaries from around the world. At the same time, over the years my eyes have been opened to the potency of "the restrictive conditions of life tied to" peoples' intercultural relationships and identity.

While in Kampala, Uganda, in 2009, both Kristen (my lovely bride) and I volunteered at a school where we were joined by a group of short-term missionaries. Jodi (her real name has been changed) was a happy-go-lucky, self-professed social justice hipster millennial from the United States. She asked me whether it was safe for her to go out in the community to take photos of children. As is always a habit of mine, I went ahead to inquire why she wanted to photograph the Ugandan children? She replied by claiming that it was part of a social justice class project she was taking in college back in the United States. I proceeded to ascertain as to whether she was doing formal research

11. Ibid., 26.
12. Steele, *Whistling Vivaldi*, 3.
13. Ibid.

and if so, whether she had inquired about the necessary protocols needed for approval. Jodi's photography endeavor turned out to be informal and for a casual post-trip presentation. The area in which Jodi wanted to stroll and take photos was located in the rural outskirts of Kampala, the capital city of Uganda. I decided to be supportive to Jodi's cause and encouraged her to make sure that she respectfully sought permission from people before taking their photos. This is a good habit to practice anywhere.

Most Ugandans are agreeable to taking their photographs, but with the influx of foreign visitors, they have become leery of poverty voyeurism, or what a friend who I met in Cape Town, South Africa, termed "poverty tourists." During Jodi's photography adventure, a six-year-old Ugandan kid walked up to her with a grin on his face and uttered the words, "Alo muzungu (hello white person)." Jodi quickly turned around as though someone had insulted her; she was red in the face and yelled back, "Hello mudugavu (black person)." Jodi was upset. We both stood in awkward silence. She apologized and felt bad for her outburst, but further expressed her resentment of the label muzungu. Actually, Jodi is not alone.

I have seen many visitors from the West wearing T-shirts that rebut the stereotype with the phrase, "My name is not muzungu." Had she been oriented about the common occurrence of the frequent reminder she would encounter with the historical social identity label of "muzungu?" Could it be that Jodi felt restricted by being called "a white person" almost everywhere she went? Is she becoming awakened to being "white" in Uganda, in a way she wasn't in the United States? I was taken aback by the situation. Jodi had been in the country for less than a year. Didn't Jodi know, as Carl Thompson narrates, that travel "involves an encounter between self and other that is brought about by movement through space . . . and of the negotiation between similarity and difference that it entailed."[14]

For both Jodi and Fikkert, there was a worry that is upsetting and distractive in their intercultural setting of confirming group based negative stereotypes relevant to their racial and ethnic identity. Their responses, although different in expression at this stage, similarly unveil injustice and privilege while targeting and negatively affecting Ugandans with a "blame the victim" tactic for not knowing better.

I believe that it is imperative for people who are interested in international missions to consider and explore the effects of stereotype threat, which is a well-studied process.

14. Thompson, *Travel Writing*, 10.

Stereotype threat between Ugandan and American missionaries

According to Claude Steele, stereotype threat "arises when one is in a situation or doing something for which a negative stereotype about one's group applies."[15] Here I insist that in missions and partnership situations between Ugandans and Americans—where exposure to negative stereotypic attitudes exists about certain communities—people with particular group identities are liable to experience stereotype threat, and therefore exhibit negative responses in their participation. The ability to detect stereotype threat in global missions in order to create an environment wherein participants who are created in the image of God are not under threat is key.

This is particularly crucial for missions pastors, leaders of short-term missions teams, and leaders of missions organizations as they design and implement intercultural curricula. Additionally, the incorporation of stereotype threat in the missions' educational undertaking is helpful in establishing the comprehension of issues like fear of the foreigner, self-doubt, social mistrust, suppression of emotions, distancing, avoidance, and other negative reactions in intercultural and interethnic mission settings.

Critical assumptions

Partnerships between Ugandan churches and American mission organizations and churches happen on a regular basis. They are formed in the commonality of theological beliefs, denominational connections, project interests, and managerial and operational agreements. Matters concerning social identities and the intercultural situational contingencies that contribute to cross-cultural conflicts are seldom addressed. Here are some salient considerations for reflection relevant in the conversation of stereotype threat in global church interactions:

- The formation of cross-cultural and transnational mission-related partnerships between Ugandan Christians and American evangelicals is influenced by social identity in various cultural settings.

- The ability to grasp the importance of social identity related challenges can help move the focus of missions preparation beyond the concerns about elements like cultural shock, the initial stress associated with a

15. Steele, "Threat in the Air," 614.

desire to "train African pastors or African leaders," claims of lack of ownership in missions projects and desired outcomes from the "locals," claims of backwardness of indigenous people, and logistical and managerial approaches, which tend to be the dominant reasons for cross-cultural conflict.

- The conflict and distances seen between well-intentioned Western missionaries and hospitable Ugandan Christians is not fictitious and should not be ignored.
- There is something "in the air"[16] of global church missions and the partnership formation atmosphere.
- The message of Jesus Christ delivers hope for global missions partnerships where gospel ambassadors can not only try to participate in reconciliation, but also always affirm one another with God's love (Rom 5; Rom 12; Phil 2:1–5).

Intercultural relationships in local and international contexts happen on a daily basis. One's ability to steer and cross cultural lines intellectually, emotionally, and culturally calls for certain degrees of intentional awareness and effort. The transition and adaptation that are needed during both short- and long-term missions experiences in a partnership between Ugandans and Americans calls for time, respectful attitudes, and perseverance.

People possess cultural backgrounds that emerge and interface in both their private and public spaces. Such is the case when missionaries who travel to Uganda (or any other country) for any length of time have relocated to new environments and situations in which they will draw on their own individual cultural perspectives. Curtis Keim ably articulates what the transitional and adaptation experience can look like. He observes that the societies we grow up in construct whole fields of memories that tell us what the world is and what it means. For example, although you might think a tree is a tree, the ways trees are used and what trees mean differ from one memory system to the next—from one culture to another. People's actions are informed by the logical and emotional behavior that deeply shaped their memory, so different cultures prefer different behaviors. When missionaries encounter something new, they tend to reach into their memories to find analogies or metaphors that allow them to categorize and make sense of the new experience.[17]

16. Ibid.

17. Keim, *Mistaking Africa*, 145.

For example, consider the story of Dana and Tim. A church in the United States prepared Dana and Tim through its mission strategy and cross-cultural training program to send them to Uganda as missionaries. The husband and wife team were assigned to join a partner church in Uganda to facilitate leadership and discipleship meetings. When they arrived, the pastor of the Ugandan church introduced the missionaries during a Sunday church gathering and made an announcement inviting and encouraging Ugandans in the congregation to get acquainted with Dana and Tim. The Ugandan congregation welcomed the American missionaries with great hospitality and expressed eagerness to help them settle in, assisting Dana and Tim while they embarked on teaching their students Western etiquette, ideas, and theology in an attempt to share their perspective.

Before giving their Ugandan students Bible study and theological assignments, Dana and Tim emphatically announced that those who did well would be rewarded with special items they had brought from the United States. However, their Ugandan counterparts did not show interest in programs the US missionaries were advertising. The American evangelical missionaries were puzzled by the lack of enthusiastic responses to their ideas and Bible studies by the Ugandan Christians present at the meeting. The missionaries sought to make some changes by learning how to effectively communicate cross-culturally from other American missionaries they met in Uganda. For example, when Tim and Dana learned of the fact that Ugandans tend to use witty proverbial statements that lend illustration from nature, the missionaries devised a plan.

The couple decided to write a discipleship study guide in the English language since English is commonly used in certain parts of the country. They incorporated drawings of various animals and local sceneries in Uganda and Africa on each page. Some of the Ugandans approached the missionaries to suggest other ways that are culturally important and even mutually helpful to both the locals and the American missionaries. In fact, some of the Christian Ugandans complained that the American missionaries' teaching sessions were "too Westernized" and disrespectful, and that it undermined the local Ugandan cultural ways. They were disappointed that Dana and Tim insisted on teaching with such an approach.

Still, Dana and Tim rejected the ideas of their Ugandan counterparts and insisted on doing missions their way, which is what Duane Elmer, author of *Cross-Cultural Conflict: Building Relationships for Effective Ministry*, calls "the win-lose strategy."[18] When the American missionaries attempted to distribute their material to different churches and volunteered to offer similar ministry training sessions like the one mentioned, their efforts did not materialize. Subsequently, Tim asserted, "Ugandans cannot think and cannot be trusted" in general.

The missionaries felt defeated and wondered why Ugandan Christians were intellectually unable to understand their approach and the ministry intended to serve the Ugandans. Needless to say, Tim's words offended Ugandans who heard his contemptuous stereotypes toward them, since some Ugandans were already familiar with such claims from some previous missionaries. At one point, one woman lamented, "They are mistreating us because we are Africans." What is the problem in this case? Is there a factor in the cross-cultural situation between the American missionaries and the Ugandans for which amenable intervention is possible?

What is the hurdle to overcome?

Unfortunately, the imploded relationships and the collateral damage in the scenario above are all too common in both short- and long-term local and global missiological experiences. The desire to build partnerships seems to be surrounded with an ambiguous notion of relationships and social capital even to the degree of fetishization in cross-cultural missions. It is expedient to talk about value and strength of "relationships," but establishing positive relationships requires missionaries from any culture nexus to have an acute alertness about stereotype threat. Understandably, since the practice of love has its difficulties, it is tempting to approach relationship building with piecemeal methods that "shoot first and ask questions later." However, such simplistic determinations are not helpful in understanding the complexity of relationships and their cultural environments in missions.

As a way forward, this book attempts to shine a beam of light on the importance of "social stereotypes,"[19] their impact, and antidotes in missions. With social stereotypes in intercultural contexts in missions, comes the prevalent issues of "a particular kind of identity contingency; that of stereotype threat."[20] Identity, contingencies are settings in cross-cultural

---

18. Elmer, *Cross-Cultural Conflict*, 34.

19. Ibid.

20. Steele, *Whistling Vivaldi*, 5.

global church moments in which a person is treated according to a specific social identity.[21]

To explain further, Professor Steele, who is the originator of the stereotype threat theory and a professor in the Department of Psychology and the Graduate School of Education at theUniversity of California Berkeley writes:

> I believe stereotype threat is a standard predicament of life. It springs from our human powers of intersubjectivity—the fact that as members of society we have a pretty good idea of what other members of our society think about lots of things, including the major groups and identities in society.[22]

Stereotype threat is prevalent in intercultural missions and the threat is evidently "rooted in concrete situations."[23] It is also necessary here to state the distinction between general stereotypes, which are not the main element of discussion in this book. On the other hand, stereotype threat theory and its ramifications in intercultural and international missions are the issues to which we will give undivided interest, even though it is undeniable that stereotypes certainly belong to the universe of stereotype threat theory. According to Shneider, stereotypes are common in culture and societies and can be defined as follows:

> The word "stereotype" itself comes from the conjunction of two Greek words: stereos, meaning "solid," and typos, meaning "the mark of a blow," or more generally "a model." Stereotypes thus ought to refer to solid models, and indeed the initial meaning of the term in English referred to a metal plate used to print pages.[24]

In fact, a variety of cultural contexts will have competing views about people's attitudes towards stereotypes. Schneider relatively argues that in particular moments it is difficult to have a clear sense of what stereotypes are. This also makes it challenging to at times differentiate how stereotypes differ from ordinary generalizations, and it is also not clear that they can or even should be avoided. To give up our capacity to form stereotypes, we would probably have to give up our capacity to generalize.[25]

21. Steele, "Steele Discusses Stereotype Threat."
22. Steele, *Whistling Vivaldi*, 5.
23. Steele, "Steele Discusses Stereotype Threat."
24. Schneider, *Psychology of Stereotyping*, 8.
25. Ibid.

Given the fluidity that surrounds stereotypes, the question that awaits exploration is timely. Can stereotype threat theory provide a process of discerning, understanding, and alleviating some of the relational issues in interethnic and transnational missional events?

As mentioned previously, Elmer explains that during a workshop for about sixty North American mission executives where the theme was "education for missionaries," the number one issue was, without question: the greatest problem in missions is relational breakdowns.[26] It is necessary to add that the consideration of situational dynamics in which relationships are strangled matter immensely. People and their relationships are inextricably intertwined with their sociocultural situations. This study has Ugandans and Americans who are seeking to partner in global missions with stereotype threat at the center. One may object that Jesus is supposed to be the sole attraction in missions: is He not enough? Indeed, Jesus and the gospel are the centrality of God's mission.

Scripture affirmatively asserts, "He is before all things, and in him all things hold together" (Col 1:17; 1 Cor 15:28). In the same manner, the tri-une God has intended, invited, and desired his followers to participate in the world of cultures. But with a spiritual and sociocultural mandate, it is noteworthy to reckon that Jesus called (Matt 4:18–22; Mark 1:16–34; Luke 5:1–11), trained (Matt 11:1; Mark 10:28–31), commissioned (Mark 3:14–19), and sent his disciples to participate in God's mission in relationally respectful and sustainable ways (Matt 22:37–40, 28:19–20; John 17:18, 20:21).

In reference to Tim and Dana and other stories presented and their association to stereotype threat, the risks are high for the proper construction of friendship and interdependent partnerships. It is necessary for followers of Christ to dwell in mutuality. Taking a closer look at the scriptures' importance and the desire for unity, friendship, solidarity, and healthy partnerships for the purpose of a fruitful witness of the gospel in missions, is at the core of Jesus' message. From Jesus' prayer, John writes,

> I pray also for those who will believe in me through their message, that all of them may be one, Father, just as you are in me and I am in you. May they also be in us so that the world may believe that you have sent me.[27]

---

26. Ibid., 33.
27. John 17:20–21.

Scripture endorses unity and love among Christ's ambassadors of the gospel, yet how are people who are interested in global and intercultural missions supposed to share the gospel of redemption and reconciliation without reflecting on the core reconciliatory values of Jesus' message? Arguably, it is possible that Tim's offensive statement was unintentional. However, this conversation does not adequately address matters of intentionality; rather, it highlights the significance of impact, and how to redress negative consequences and prevent them.

It is significant to recognize that even in the absence of perfect intentions, real consequences abound for human interaction in missions. Case in point, Tim's statements create a lingering negative stigma that is directed at the people they have an opportunity to serve. To state that Africans don't and can't think for themselves or even be trusted is counter to a gospel response and an understanding of respect, gentleness, and the fact that God, who is the origin of missions, equally creates humans. In the course of over twenty years of intercultural global work, I have heard phrases like, "I have my orphan in Africa. We teach the Africans how to run a meeting. We are teaching African mothers how to breastfeed. They don't understand how to do accounting our way. Who will take care of the orphans when we (short-termers) leave? They don't know how to dig wells or bore holes. They don't know how to serve food at a banquet. Africans have failed to take ownership of 'our' missions and humanitarian ideas and programs."

One missionary queried to me about "how un-Christian it is for Christian couples in Uganda not to display public affection like they did back at home in the West." In a certain post on Facebook, a short-term mission trooper, wrote, "documenting the faces, the sights, the colors . . . It's been a great trip discovering Rwanda and her people!" Yes, technology has afforded us global access to any and all information. I even took a snapshot of the message on Facebook, thanks to smart cameras. You can add your own to this list. We are also used to receiving overzealous social justice short-term Christian humanitarians who end up feeling frustrated and defeated. Although not from Uganda, here is an example that directly captures how missionary frustrations, deferred assumptions and hopes are expressed at times. According to one social justice volunteer,

> I believed that if Guatemalan children needed a school, then the local church could open one. . . . How should we have balanced the need to address institutional injustice, the children's educational needs, and the fact that challenging government corruption could

take years? Unfortunately, we did not know any . . . Guatemalan brothers and sister who were wrestling with these issues.[28]

Really? Do you find such an assertion plausible? That there was no one in Guatemala with whom the American Christian short-term missions team member could work with? Is it true that there are no Guatemalan families that aren't aware of the need of education for the children and aren't working toward a local long-term solution? Perhaps the American short-terms weren't patient enough to look for Guatemalan brothers and sisters, because there are plenty of capable Guatemalans who are heavily involved in caring from their communities. Here again, the assumptions of the American short-term mission project and its unstated implications of passivity, failure, and fatalism levied on the personality and identity of Guatemalans. They are represented as helplessly absent local victims, whose obvious suffering can only be identified by the prevailing foreign missionary.

In the case of both Dana and Tim, they implicated themselves in a self-defeating situation. Due to their approach, they are also vulnerable to the missed opportunity to learn how the gospel uniquely manifests and relates with the broader Ugandan cultural experiences. It is a case of well-intended desires, but unintended consequences. Conceivably, unbeknownst to Tim, and Dana by association, they stereotypically impose conditions on the Ugandan cultural, social, and spiritual identities, which interplay with contingencies also involved in building potentially friendly and interdependent partnerships in God's global mission.

It is understandable that looking into the Ugandan cultural terrain can provide some further insights into the tenuous problems of intercultural missions partnership than stereotype threat. Such a notion has been a staple suspicion in cross-cultural missions. However, the challenge is that in missions between the West and Africa, African culture by and large tends to be viewed negatively. About those attitudes, Bediako notes that Christian missionaries often opposed or denigrated traditional local customs and institutions, as well as traditional tribal ceremonies and authority systems.[29] The extent to which cultures may have causal bearing on cross-cultural conflict is a subject for another occasion.

Yet, a clear challenge with the castigation of African culture is its one-sided perspective given that cultural imperfections are common to all human cultures. It is even thinkable that both Tim's reaction and the Ugandans'

28. Offutt et al., *Advocating for Justice*, 6–7.

29. Bediako, *Christianity in Africa*, 26.

collective disengaged response largely stems from antecedent conditions. Yet, a research study about stereotype threat and the intellectual test performance of African Americans conducted by Steele and Aronson points to "the immediate situational threat . . . "[30] as worthy of attention. In cross-cultural missions, it necessary to redress the menaces that emerge in a situation and not assumes that relational challenges will subside on their own. According to Steele and Aronson, vigilant efforts need to be directed to the

> threat that derives from the broad dissemination of negative stereotype about one's group—the threat of possibly judged and treated stereotypically, or of possibly self-fulfilling such a stereotype.[31]

Where do stereotypes come from and how do people who desire to contribute to the common good across cultures acquire the ability to categorize fellow humanity? Stereotypes are part and parcel of our socialization processes. Now, due to the limited scope of this book, this conversation does not attempt to discuss the causal questions and gaps at the biological and genetic level, but will extend the idea of social stereotype threat in the global church missions contexts.

If Dana and Tim have learned the negative stereotypical responses during their childhood and coming-of-age socialization periods, are they to blame for messages they co-opted? I don't think so, since it is also most likely the actions were unintentional. It is possible they assumed that their way of communication was universal, without taking into consideration the situational threats and the impact of negative stereotypes in global church partnerships and missions. While they might not be at fault for the stereotypes, distortions, and omissions that shaped their thinking, they are not relieved from the responsibility of their actions.[32] Evidently, their ways go beyond mundane linguistic slips and the possibility of misspoken attempts. Their assertions reveal the shortsightedness of their cross-cultural practices and negative stereotypical attitudes perhaps rooted in the pervasive American images of Africans in general. Tim and Dana's perspective is disadvantageous to the spiritual and sociocultural identification of their Ugandan counterparts.

Incidentally, Dana and Tim are adversely impacted by their situations in ways that hinder their ability to engage in the process of trust development.

---

30. Steele and Aronson, "Stereotype Threat and the Intellectual Test," 798.

31. Ibid.

32. Tatum, *Why Are All*, 7.

The Ugandan responses to stereotypes asserting inferior ability and untrustworthiness about their group present a fact called "stereotype threat." The social and cross-cultural stress created reinforces the effects of stereotype threat in missions. The Ugandans' intellectual and trustworthy credibility, which is salient, is not only attacked, they are left in a state of morass. In a study about reducing the effects of stereotype threat, Aronson, Fried, and Good, observe that people negatively impacted by stereotype threat

> bear an extra cognitive and emotional burden not borne by people for whom the stereotype does not apply. This burden takes the form of a performance-disruptive apprehension, anxiety about the possibility of conforming to a deeply negative racial inferiority—in the eyes of others, in one's own eyes, or both at the same time. Importantly, it is not necessary that a student believe the stereotype to feel this burden.[33]

Notably, the story above does not reveal the possible existing negative cultural stereotypes that Ugandans have about Americans, but that does not mean that they do not exist. For example, according to data from a recent survey conducted, Ugandans use the term muzungu to describe America missionaries and Western expatriates. Other stereotypes associated with North American Christians from the surveys completed by Ugandans include "law abiding,[34] "rich, self-assured, intelligent, enterprising, military experts, happy . . . [and] liberal."[35] Ugandan participants also noted that certain American short-term missionaries "do not know world geography."[36] The interviewees who are also Americans expressed the following stereotypes about Ugandans. One American participant noted:

> I would say my perception has been that they are poor, hungry, simple, in need. Ha! Yes. My preconceived notions of Africans fell hard my first semester of graduate school when I realized that my East African classmates were highly intelligent, wealthy, capable, and funnier than me.[37]

33. Aronson, Fried, and Good, "Reducing the Effects of Stereotype Threat," 114.

34. Peace Apiyo, interview by the author, June 6, 2014, Kampala, Uganda.

35. John Muhumuza, interview by the author, January 14, 2014, Kampala, Uganda.

36. Peace Apiyo, interview by the author, June 6, 2014, Kampala, Uganda.

37. Matthew Johnson, interview by the author, March 15, 2015, Vancouver, Washington.

In reference to the existence of negative stereotypes, Schipper correspondingly presents evidence that African literature bears witness to stereotype information about the colonial muzungu. Schipper writes,

> Their rude behavior is uncivilized, they steal (emptying Africa of its riches); they are lazy (Africans do all the work for them and are paid very little). And, what kind of civilization does the West have as a continent that counts two destructive world wars among its achievements?

Even more poignant to anyone who might have entertained Fikkert's idea of not helping but "letting," and therefore squeezing out resources from Africans living in abject poverty (who might not be aware that they should help until a Westerner writes about it), instead of a wealthy person like him choosing to help, Schipper further notes:

> The image of the white man, just like its counterpart, consists of numerous observations that are indicative of mistrust and misunderstandings, dividing. . . . The most striking thing about the [Bazungu] characters in a number of African novels . . . is that they exhibit pathological greed: they are eternally hungry for more money. The god of the [Bazungu] lives in their wallets, one of the authors observes, which is why "in God we trust" is written on their money.[38]

Again, it is clear that the statements above are stereotypes, but the double tragedy in the mind-set of "when helping hurts" is it plays right into those already existing negative assumptions at the expense of demonstrating gospel-centric compassion, generosity, and empathy.

With the obvious presence of preconceived ideas about one another, it is crucial to take a closer look at how stereotype threat affects interethnic missions in the global church. Since understanding stereotype threat theory is strategic in the global church's endeavors in the process of partnership formation between Ugandans and Americans, the definition of stereotype threat is fitting. We must ask ourselves, what is the global impact?

38. Schipper, *Imagining Insiders*, 39.

Chapter 4

Go to All the Nations! Ready, Steady, Go!

SHORT-TERM MISSIONS ARE THE primary gateway for intercultural experiences and transferences, both of resources and of relational interactions within the global Christian family. A staggering amount of people from churches in the United States travel on short-term missions trips every year. According to Baylor University, "The number of United States Christians taking part in trips lasting a year . . . has grown from 540 in 1965 to an estimated more than 1.5 million annually, with an estimated $2 billion per year spent on the effort."[1] Due to the ongoing and growing interest in the idea of Christian evangelical short-termism characterized by missions groups that travel to Uganda and other countries for one and a half weeks on average, American missions continue to boom. Long-term missions, and the desire to create global church partnerships remain steady and this dialogue seeks to discuss the necessary awareness of the stereotype threat in interethnic and intercultural missions as a key dynamic between an evangelical church in Uganda and a church group in the United States.

This dialogue is distinguishable because it does not solely focus on the missionary as a self-contained and independent cross-culture unit to be filled with intercultural information only; this body of work elevates and adheres to the "power of the situation."[2] The power of situation also has a lot to do with how the power systems work in a situation and community. For the most part in global missions, the structural plane between

1. "Short-Term Mission Trips: Are They Worth the Investment?"

2. Inzlicht and Schmader, *Stereotype Threat*, 7. The power of the situation alludes to the appealing consequence of this situational approach, which highlights the importance of studying the situation in which stereotype threat is operative and thus intervention designed to remove negative effects of stereotype threat can change the situation in which targeted groups find themselves.

Western missions and Africa are systemically uneven when it comes to the particular brand of missions requiring international travel. I have also been curious and still find it inquisitive that the short-term and long-term missionary profession and vocation is unidirectional. By far, most missionaries invaded in short-term missions and long-term career missions are not from Africa. What I mean by this is that "the United States still tops the chart by far in terms of total missionaries, sending 127,000 in 2010 compared to the 34,000 sent by No. 2-ranked Brazil."[3]

I am tempted to comparatively study the nature of dynamics involved in search of a high turnout of American Christian missions and American Olympic teams since both come out on top: one with a high sent missionary count, the other with the highest medals awarded in the recent Olympic games. Could it be the benefits of a powerful free-market economy and a high competitive spirit? What exactly? Although an adequate response to such inquires are beyond this discussion, it is helpful to observe that the manner in which societies are organized tend to influence cultural representations and experiences. The global missions arena is impacted by stereotype threat as a condition of life because of the way cultures are "organized around . . . identity."[4] Even though the identification of stereotype threat does not preclude other factors that could also contribute to interethnic challenges in missions, it leads to a situational approach with dramatically altered and simple interventions designed to remove those threats[5] as will be discussed in chapter 9. Cross-cultural missions and the resulting local and global relationships are bound to issues of ethnic and race orientation, culture, and social identity. The element of identity is a fundamental issue when it comes to intercultural partnerships in missions between Ugandan and American churches. According to Steele, identity *contingence* is the thing you have to deal with in a situation because you have a given social identity: you are a white male, a woman, black, Latino, and so on. Generally speaking, contingencies are circumstances you have to deal with in order to get what you want or need in a situation."[6]

Does identity matter to intercultural missions between Ugandans and American Christians? Further still, is America not a post-racial society with the historical passage of the civil rights act and two-time election

---

3. Steffan, "Surprising Countries."

4. Steele, *Whistling Vivaldi*, 3.

5. Ibid.

6. Ibid.

of Barack Obama—the first African America president? And is Uganda a postcolonial society? Although still debatable, both societies have demonstrated advancements toward attainable levels of human freedoms and rights. Steele argues, however, that even with some earned progress,

> things have gotten better. But remember, contingencies grow out of an identity's role in the history and organization of a society—its role in the DNA of a society—and how society has stereotyped that identity. In the case of race in the United States, that history and its legacies are still with us. . . . Research . . . shows, the stereotype and identity threats that can arise in today's racially integrated colleges—especially those with an accumulation of identity-threatening cues—can be formidable, not as diminishing of life chances as the total exclusion of yesteryear, but an unfortunate suppression of human potential nonetheless.[7]

The disparity that exists between the majority and minority culture in the United States continues to point to the laments and brutal repercussions of racism's past and its systemic effects today. The ongoing unrest can be seen in the tensions between the police's use of force in communities of color. Intensity in the United States' domestic racial situation is also evident in the dispute about historical policies of inequality. According to Darity and Frank, there is a lively debate today about the given suitability of reparations to compensate First Nations Peoples' colonial setbacks due to disenfranchisement, and African Americans for having been subjected to slavery.[8]

In Uganda, stereotypic language about one's tribe is usually invoked in society, and some of the stereotype threats based on tribal lines also proved advantageous during Western imperial efforts in Uganda. The backdrop of such sentiments go way back to Western colonial expansion, because the British employed tribal agents of their imperialism, and a policy that was often referred to as tribal sub-imperialism.[9] Stereotype threat can have hostile implications on any given society as this book seeks to illuminate. The following section will examine some of the past and present dynamics involved in the attempts of American evangelicals and Ugandan Christians to work together regarding stereotype threats.

---

7. Ibid., 212–13.

8. Darity and Frank, "Economics of Reparations," 326–29.

9. Mutibwa, *Uganda Since Independence*, 3.

A biblically contextual and practical application for the mitigation of stereotype threat in the interest of working toward faithful friendships and interdependent partnerships will be proposed. In that direction, the negative outlook of Africa as the "dark continent" that has lingered in missions narratives or the questions about the validity of sending US missionaries, this book consistently calls for attention to the impact of stereotype threat at the expense of solidarity in missions. The increasing flow of mission groups from the United States that frequently travel to Uganda and the East African region continues to attract American interest. Curiously, East Africa is one of the most evangelized parts of the world, so what are the missionaries going to do? In my conversations I have been told by many short termers of their disgruntlement of going to Africa just to hold babies. But again, it seems to show that they are running into the empty promises of stereotypes.

News and the economic possibilities in the African continent are slowly drawing the attention of nations around the world. The president of the United States, while on a visit to Kenya, affirmed his interest in the region, "because Africa is on the move. Africa is also one of the fastest-growing regions of the world."[10] Every year, international airports are flooded with various missions and tourist groups, predominately from the Western world, in transit to different cultures of the world. Missions t-shirts are easy to spot and come in all colors, red and yellow, black and white, they are precious in our sight. We get our identity from our mission colors and want to heal the world. But in our branded mission t-shirts and their symbolism are we aware of the stereotypic impact they have on the missionizers and the missionized?

Missiological interest in this case continues to exist between Christians in Uganda and churches in the United States. However, as the different cultures meet, there are relational complications that tend to fuel conflict and divisions between Ugandans and American evangelicals. The global church space is where intercultural mission activities often happen, and it is also a place where there are both similarities and differences among cultures, races, and ethnicities. Along with that are the highly likely possibilities that followers of Jesus will also encounter stereotype threats as they sojourn across cultures with the desire to seek partnerships. Rosenthal, Crisp, and Suen, in their study on reducing stereotype threat, "Predicted that placing participants under conditions conductive of stereotype threat would result in these participants predicting lower performance expectancies."[11]

10. "Remarks by President Obama at the Global Entrepreneurship Summit."
11. Rosenthal, Crisp, and Suen, "Improving Performance Expectancies," 588.

When leaders of missions organizations fail to be mindful of the preventable cues of stereotype threat in the volunteer and missionary preparatory processes, there will be relational confusion. Additionally, too often cross-cultural discussions in missions have a limited focus on proper dress, culture shock, accents, and how to exchange money. Helpful as those may be, the pivotal idea in this book will seek to contribute to missiology by raising consciousness about the impact of stereotype threat in global church interactions. Paying serious attention to the vast veil of stereotype threat that prevents an awakened conscience about the peril of identity stigma in missions is paramount in the twenty-first century.

The alertness and respect toward people's humanity and dignity in missional relationships between Ugandan Christians and American evangelicals is critical to both parties. When Ugandan and American Christians meet, there are assumptions about unity because of shared commonality in their professed Christian identity. Also, the expectation of togetherness is recorded in the Christian scriptures, such that Paul writes, "Love each other with brotherly affection and take delight in honoring each other."[12]

Other points of contact lay in the religious and cultural worldview of Ugandans, who do not separate religious, societal, and cultural life, but rather consider life as a total sum. American evangelicals involved in missions in Uganda tend to uphold a similar disposition. According to Amstutz, American missionaries tend toward "caring for the spiritual and temporal well-being of people in foreign lands,"[13] which is in contrast to the earlier disposition of the Western mission enterprise that was "chiefly spiritual"[14] by design. The problem of ethnic stereotypes against a people's culture and self-identity, demonstrated in the opening story, is that they do not advance God's love and unity necessary in the complex issues of interculturality and global encounters in the global missions arena.

To begin with, stereotypes are present in all cultural spheres and their histories. The nature of negative stereotypes and their effects on a targeted group can be traced back to the domestic ethos in the United States. Loury, who is a professor of the social sciences and economics at Brown University, asserts,

> An awareness of the racial "otherness" of blacks is embedded in
> the social consciousness of the American nation owing to the

12. Rom 12:10.

13. Amstutz, *Evangelicals*, 50.

14. Ibid.

historical fact of slavery and its aftermath. This inherited stigma even today exerts an inhibiting effect on the extent to which African Americans can realize their full human potential.[15]

In Uganda, the known existence of ethnic-based stereotypes have their roots in the colonial legacy.[16] By and large, Uganda is a host cultural context for numerous missions-minded groups from American churches and missions organizations. Uganda's domestic culture puts a high relational value on hospitality and is therefore culturally receptive toward visitors from both within and without the culture. When both short- and long-term missionaries from a given church in America desire to forge partnerships, the awareness about the dangers of stereotype threat is necessary. Likewise, a similar enlightenment is beneficial for cross-cultural missions-minded followers of Jesus in Uganda. Why is a conversation about stereotype threat, the stigmatization of people, and its effect on global church relations critical? What is at stake?

The use of negative stereotypes is hazardous against a people's spiritual, social, and cultural identity in global missions to the detriment of faithful friendships and mutual trust in the global church. This is why an appropriate response leads to a biblical missiological perspective, which maintains the obvious belief in the global church's mandate to present the grand plan of God's purpose for his creation, people, and nations around the world. This reinforces the fact that ambassadors of the Gospel of Jesus Christ are designated adherents and messengers of the Bible's global message. Wright argues,

> If our mission is to share good news, we need to be people of good news. If we preach a gospel of transformation, we need to show some evidence of what transformation looks like. So there is a range of questions we need to ask about [the global church relations] that have to do with things like integrity, justice, unity, inclusion, and Christlikeness. The biblical word is "holiness," and it is as much a part of our missional identity as of our personal sanctification.[17]

The mission of God is guided by principles and a call for its practitioners to be widely given to humility of spirit, "respect and gentleness,"[18] as processes

---

15. Loury, *Anatomy of Racial Inequality*, 5.

16. Kyeyune, *Legacy of a Hero*, 174.

17. Wright, *Mission of God's People*, 295.

18. 1 Pet 3:15.

through which to deliver on both spiritual and social virtues opposed to neither blissful ignorance nor arrogance. Jesus Christ expressed the desired attitude needed and the reward that follows in an indelible sermon noting, "Blessed are the meek, for they shall inherit the earth."[19] A humble disposition in missions is vastly positive in contrast to the humiliation from the stigmatization of a people in the local ethnic identities and the contingences that follow thereafter.

To illustrate further, Goffman in his historical work and initial vocalization on stigma brought the subject to light in the 1960s. Goffman describes stigmas as an attribute that makes a targeted person or group different from others in the category of persons available, and such an attribute is especially discrediting in its effect.[20] It is due to the debilitating effects of such ethnocentric and negative stereotypes that a focus on their implication in the transnational context of the global church between Ugandan followers of Christ and their counterparts in America is warranted. Such attention is also made urgent by Christianity's growth and witness in the global context, particularly in the non-western context. According to Jenkins,

> We are currently living through one of the transforming moments in the history of religion worldwide. Over the last five centuries, the story of Christianity has been inextricably bound up with that of Europe and European-derived civilizations overseas, above all in North America. Until recently, the overwhelming major of Christians lived in . . . "European Christian" civilization. . . . It is self-evidently the religion of the haves. . . . Over the last century, however, the center of gravity in the Christian world has shifted inexorably away from Europe, southward, to Africa and Latin America, and eastward, toward Asia.[21]

The euphoric news about Christianity's purported expansive shift from the West to other parts of the world has attracted further affirmation. Mbiti notes, "The centers of the church's universality [are] no longer in Geneva, Rome, Athens, Paris, London, New York, but Kinshasa, Buenos Aires, Addis Ababa, and Manila."[22] The other geopolitical elements that continue to perform midwifery roles in the spread of global Christianity are globalization, which also includes the impact of foreign policies and economics. With

19. Matt 5:5.
20. Goffman, *Stigma*, 3.
21. Jenkins, *Next Christendom*, 1.
22. John Mbiti, as quoted in Bediako, *Christianity in Africa*, 154.

such dimensions also come the promises of the advancement of technology, opportunity, religious freedom, and interfaith and intergroup harmony.

Yet, even the enthusiasm with which the new growth of the global church in Uganda and Africa has been received, the missions arena still reverberates with questions. If Christianity's domain scale has tipped away from the West in favor of non-Western regions like Africa, does this also imply the end of the dominant influence of Western Christianity in the metaphorical global South? Research about the current efforts of the American evangelical missions enterprise suggest the contrary. As a matter of fact, according to *Christianity Today*, "the US still does send the largest total number of missionaries, 127,000 in 2010."[23] A reasonable number of Western missionaries have traveled to Uganda on both short- and long-term mission ventures in order to register their impact. This study is concerned with how the relationships between American missionaries and their Ugandan Christian counterparts are impacted by certain contingencies fostered by prevailing stereotype threats as shown earlier in Dana and Tim's story.

Historical narrative

In the interest of understanding the complexities surrounding the challenges caused by stereotype threat in missiological space among Christian Ugandans, non-Christian Ugandans, Christian Americans, and non-Christian Americans, it is important to look at the historical dimension that lay between the past and modern day realities. Tim, Dana, and their Uganda colleagues' dilemma can be appropriately followed through the further elucidation of the troubled and damaged past in which practice of global Christian missions environmentally plays out among the East African nation of Uganda, and in which American Christian missionaries seek to immerse themselves. To begin with a broader continental view, history shows:

> That partition of Africa introduced virulent forms of western nationalism into the continent. The Berlin Conference's demand for physical presence rather than mere declarations of areas of influence opened the African interior to missionary gaze and intervention with the character that change the cross-cultural process. Western self-confidence replaced the initial respect for African Chiefs as colonial weaponry was enormously the behest of gospel bearers. The scale of missionary activities was enormously

23. "World's Top Missionary-Sending Country."

enlarged, making analysis complex; competition among missionaries became rife: broadly, Catholics squared off against Protestants. . . . Missionary policy was forged amidst the competing claims of colonial ambitions, evangelical spirituality, and obligations to the indigenous people.[24]

Unlike conventional understandings, this study acknowledges that not all of the current challenges in cross-culture missions between Ugandans and Americans have Western colonialism to solely blame. Even with the consequences that still remain in many communities in Africa, which have their origin from imperialism, human beings are resilient. Most of the communities in Africa that experience both indirect and direct colonial rule continue to learn from the past and persist to work toward common good and a harmonious existence. It is necessary for the prevailing models of global missions to also study past events and positively glean from history. Moreover, for centuries the Western missions enterprise has and continues to hold a place of dominance through sending both short- and long-term missionaries to Uganda and not the other way round. Such disparities contribute to uneven distribution of power in cross-cultural interactions and can fuel stereotypic impressions. Cross-cultural partnerships are strained when power differentials are not equitably negotiated and represented. Could failure to examine and reflect on the implications of such historically educational events hinder Western missionaries' alertness to a Western hegemonic worldview, thus resulting in a cultural messianic complex in missions? Gilley and Stanley further write,

> The texture of colonial Christianity contained four strands that would challenge the indigenous peoples and evoke response. First, the character of the missionary presence was exhibited in such varied contexts as the mission . . . [like] the protection of the settler communities in eastern African, and the increasing rejection . . . for African agency. . . . The second strand was a cultural policy that despised indigenous realties and embedded racism in mission practice. Third, the institutionalization of mission agencies ignored the pneumatological resources of the gospel, sapped the vigor of the original evangelical spirituality and encrusted the monopoly of decision making processes and the practice of faith. Fourth, translation of the Scriptures exposed the underbelly of the missionary enterprise and produced unintended consequences.[25]

24. Gilley and Stanley, *World Christianity*, 576–77.
25. Ibid.

The depth of the impact of the four strands named above had serious and significant implications. The cultural policy, for instance, raises curiosity about particular moments in time. For purposes of reflection, during the era of transatlantic slavery, there were both its Christian proponents and opponents as well. Although Curtin's research dates back to 1973, his work is rare and still relevant for this study. Curtin ably insists on the insatiable posture of Western cultural superiority on both the pro- and anti-slavery Western wings, as he writes,

> The antislavery movement provides another illustration of the "moderate racism" that existed in the minds of early-nineteenth-century Europeans and Americans. From our perspective it seems logical that abolitionists would attempt to eliminate racism in their efforts to end slavery. But the abolitionist's arguments were primarily about the immorality of slavery and the slave trade rather than the immorality of racism. Proslavery and antislavery activists alike were racist, but both assumed that cultural factors were at the heart of the slavery question. For proponents of slavery, the African's inferior culture justified the institution. Antislavery activists argued that Christian charity required abolition and that Africans had the *potential* to acquire civilized culture.[26]

While the historical peril of the transatlantic slave trade is long gone, the global missionary context between America and Uganda still has to consider the spiritual, social, and cultural legacy of the colonial missionary era and mentality. Of the colonial missionary enterprise, Sanneh writes,

> The missionaries compounded the deeply oppressive character of colonial rule in Africa by paving the way for swift and decisive access to the hearts and minds of Africans who, ingesting the bitter pill of political defeat yielded . . . and . . . The [spread of the Christian religion] entered African culture like a tranquilizing needle and came out like the sword of domination.[27]

The above reality bears consequential implications for the African Christian's identity and global missions. The need to address the stereotype threat that plagues global church relations is urgent since stereotype threat possesses destructive outcomes to the identity of all people and groups involved in cross-cultural missions. Inzlicht and Schmader write, "People from all social groups—including those who do not belong to traditionally stereotyped

26. Curtin, *Image of Africa*, 138.
27. Sanneh, *Disciples of All Nations*, 150–51.

groups—can be affected by identity-threatening cues and experience the cognitive, behavioral, and emotional disruptions of stereotype threat."[28]

When Western missionaries fail to question the impact of the learning experiences of their past and present that have and continue to inform the learning identity of the people and cultures with whom they desire to sojourn, it is difficult for them to know the threatening cues. For example, even though the scope of this book is limited to the analysis of how Western missionaries are prepared for "culture shock," it is nonetheless revealing when the tendency to treat "culture shock" simplistically as a negative experience in the culture relegated to the "cultural other"[29] continues to be prevalent in the Western mission enterprise. Such practices are misleading and limit the Western missionaries' behavior toward other cultures with a hypercritical spirit, thereby reducing people and their culture to a factual art, and reinforcing stereotype threat.

The call for attentiveness to stereotype threat is overdue given the centuries of Western interest and involvement in the mission enterprise. According to Christian Smith, in the "nineteenth century, American evangelicals had mobilized a missionary enterprise of vast proportions that was spreading the gospel in Africa."[30] Accordingly, a large group of American Christians today are involved in transnational ministries in Uganda, which are established to help orphans, end poverty, train pastors, and plant more churches in addition to the inland churches that already exist. At any rate, the interest of missions between Ugandan and American Christians continues to steadily develop.

This is precisely why the church in North America fits this book's undertaking, more so because American Christians represent the dominant group that sends both short- and long-term missionaries to Uganda. Incidentally, American Christian evangelicals are increasingly making an imprint on the spiritual and social cultural fabric of Uganda, and not the other way around. The most recent evidence of American and Ugandan Christian interaction is the debate about the controversial Ugandan anti-homosexuality legislation—a debate that was prominently featured on the global stage.

The subject of homosexuality is beyond the scope of this study. However, for illustrative purposes, the globally strident discussion about sexuality between Uganda and the United States is enlightening. American

---

28. Inzlicht and Schmader, *Stereotype Threat*, 22.

29. Woodley, "Mission and the Cultural Other", 456.

30. Smith et al., *American Evangelicalism*, 3.

evangelicalism's impact is further sketched during Pastor Rick Warren's visit to Uganda. On Pastor Warren's tour in Uganda, it was evident that the high profile American evangelical pastor has ties in Uganda, including connections with members of Parliament. Warren's voice on the debate about homosexuality was clear in its convictions. That same year, Warren also christened Uganda a "purpose-driven country." Such influence led observers to entertain the possibility that "Africa's anti-gay campaigns are to a substantial degree made in the US."[31]

In order to understand the nature of missional partnerships between Ugandan Christians and American evangelicals, a broader overview of the situational influence of the geopolitical and historical impact of the West is fitting. The African continent has long bristled with livelihood in villages, communities, cities, and kingdoms, yet the 1880s and 1890s experienced the pains of terrifying upheaval. In a period of twenty years, almost the entire continent of Africa was balkanized by European domination. Harlow and Carter report:

> Convened in late 1884 and concluded in February of the following year, the Berlin Conference, which had been summoned by Germany's Prince Bismarck, sought to color in the map of what was commonly known as the "dark continent." According to the General Act of the Berlin Conference, Africa was to be partitioned among . . . European national contestants—Britain, France, Germany, Portugal, and Italy—and King Leopold II of Belgium [plus the United States].[32]

As though the partition was not set back enough for the African people and their continent, the Euro-American scramble for Africa was administered without any representatives and consent from Africans. Such aggression and paternalism was part and parcel of the common Western imperial competition attitude toward African people. During the period mentioned above, Europe was in the midst of the Industrial Revolution, which also coincided with Europe imperial enterprise's determination to venture on the African continent. For instance, Tvedt argues that Britain's annexation and control in Uganda was concerned with preventing other European powers, particularly Germany and France from muscling in London's economic sphere of interest.[33]

31. Ibid.

32. Carter and Harlow, *Archives of Empire*, 1.

33. Tvedt, "Hydrology and Empire," 173–94.

Europe's presence in Africa transformed the existing cities and civilizations into the workshop of the world. Although some of Western missionary ventures in certain parts of the African continent began before formal imperialism, the age of the race for Africa by imperialistic powers was linked with European missionary exploration. Robert asserts that the burgeoning British Empire was the context in which most Western Protestant missionaries worked and that Africa, the work of Western missionary groups, typically preceded imperial interest.[34] The nature of the relationship between missions and the establishment of the Western empire continues to be a source of debate in missiological circles.

The times of Western colonial expansion and the partitioned African territories were sources marked by the extraction of raw materials: gold, diamonds, cash crops, and eventually slaves. It was the dawn of industrial-scale production, modern capitalist economies, and mass international trade. In this new industrial era, the value of Africa as a place for extraction of natural and human resource skyrocketed. Its strategic trade routes and wholesale market for the goods Europe produced was ideal. Nonetheless, the scramble for Africa was not just a quest for economic vitality in the Western world; European expansion through imperialism and colonialism also became the fast track to political supremacy in Europe and the spread of Western Christianity. How did the large-scale and hasty undertaking of European conquest in the African region emerge? It began with the loud call of a renowned missionary and explorer, Dr. David Livingstone, whose ambition among many was to pave a "Missionary Road"—"God's Highway," he also called it—1,500 miles north into the interior to bring "Christianity and civilization" to unreached peoples.[35]

Even though David Livingstone's mission activities on the African continent might have galvanized Western missionary interest, they also produced other consequences. History further shows:

> Each responded to Livingstone's call in his own fashion. But they
> all conceived of the crusade in terms of romantic nationalism.
> There were journalist-explorers like Henry Stanley, sailor-explorers like Pierre de Brazza, soldier-explorers like Frederick Lugard,
> pedagogue-explorers like Carl Peters, gold-and-diamond tycoons
> like Cecil Rhodes. Most of them were outsiders of one kind or
> another but no less ardent nationalists for that. To imperialism—a

---

34. Robert, *Converting Colonialism*, 10.
35. Galli, *131 Christians Everyone Should Know*, 248.

kind of "race patriotism"—they brought a missionary zeal. Not only would they save Africa from itself. Africa would be the saving of their own countries.[36]

In the interest of discussing the relationship between Ugandan Christians and American evangelicals in missions, it is worth an attempt to unravel the limitations that have encumbered the possibility of healthy dialogue interactions of a church in Portland, Oregon, and its counterpart in Uganda. There are common views about the way of life of Ugandans that pervade the minds of American missionaries who continue to envisage themselves working in many countries as an expression of their faith.

Along with general views, Americans Christians seem to possess desires to be involved in changing situations that seem to impede on certain freedoms of humanity beyond the Americas. For example, Amstutz shows that American evangelical anticommunism expressed support for victims of religious persecution. Since freedom of religion was curtailed in communist regimes, the National Association of Evangelicals (NAE), the informal association of some forty-five evangelical denominations, adopted several resolutions expressing concern about rising religious persecution.[37] Along such a backdrop, many American Christians are involved with ministries in Uganda, which are established to help orphans, end poverty, train pastors, and plant more churches. However, the non-American missionary presence has also been in existence as well. For example, in Uganda, Ugandans propagated the gospel. According to Hastings:

> Buganda is the only place in Africa where there was both large-scale conversions to Christianity in the pre-colonial era and a mass conversion movement within the early colonial age. The latter was most certainly dependent upon the former, and while the arrival of British rule in the early 1890s facilitated it, the explanation for what happened is to be found less in any colonial logic than in the initial conversions and stormy events of the 1880s, leading up to the political and military triumph of the Christian minority in a situation when British rule was certainly not anticipated, at least upon the African side.[38]

The above demonstration of non-Western involvement in the spread of Christianity is part of a renaissance rooted in the validation of Ugandan Christians'

36. Pakenham, *Scramble for Africa*, xxii.
37. Amstuz, *Evangelicals and American Foreign Policy*, 3.
38. Hastings, *Church in Africa*, 464.

role as participants in God's global mission. In American evangelical missiological circles, there is a prevalent understanding that is celebratory of "bringing or taking" the gospel of Jesus Christ to Uganda and the African continent. However, with the earlier evidence noted of the God-given ability of Ugandan Christians to effectively serve their communities through the dissemination of the gospel, it is clear that God's message of human redemption has always been present before the arrival of American missionaries.

Additionally, it makes sense that American Christians who possess inclinations toward missionary work in Uganda seek to establish mutual trust with their non-Western counterparts in Uganda for global missions work. Such an expectation is also necessary for Ugandan missionaries, but the fundamental difference lays in the fact that very few, if any, Ugandan evangelicals participate in global short or long-term missionary work in the Western sense, compared to their American Christian counterparts. Yet, even through the recognition of the Ugandan and African in the church's role in world Christianity continues to gain visibility, by and large, there are challenges in global missions that need attention. A closer examination is warranted regarding the mission endeavors of the North American church, since the American evangelical enterprise's interest and distribution of missions groups globally remains steady. Here, I will give an in-depth look at the assumptions of American Christian missionaries who sojourn on both short- and long-term trips to Uganda. The gravitas of the proposed vigilance is heightened by observers like Kristof who writes of "a broad new trend that is beginning to reshape American foreign policy: America's evangelicals have become the newest [informal international ambassadors]."[39]

Albeit, the mixture of American evangelicals and American foreign policy is a curious one and therefore casts the need to further inquire about what qualifies certain American evangelicals to fit the title of American foreign policy representatives, a question for another kind of book. Yet, if American evangelicals are agents of their nationalistic values, ideas, and interests, does this also mean that they are transporters of American ideologies and cultural assumptions? It is possible that the forces behind American Christian internationalists and their assumptions that come to bear during missionary attempts in Uganda have their connection in the socioeconomic and political context in America as well. According to Schulzinger:

> American foreign policy since the Spanish-American War of 1898
> has sought to ensure US supremacy in the Western Hemisphere

39. Kristof, "Following God Abroad."

while at the same time asserting American influence widely around the globe. . . . Since 1900, most officials in charge of setting American foreign policy have consistently sought to engage the United States deeply in political and economic affairs beyond the water's edge. But officials do not act alone. Outside the executive branch, members of Congress, the press, and well-spoken and influential private citizens have all sought to set the direction of the United States in foreign affairs.[40]

Suggestively, American evangelicals in their posture of "internationalist" are not only emissaries of an American Christian message, but they are also diplomats of their customs, interests, and assumptions. Could the claims of the supposed assumptions be baseless since it is possible that some evangelical Americans with interest in missions do in fact posses certain information about life in Uganda? Undoubtedly, there are a handful of studious and informed individuals who will take to the acquisition of the necessary context for their missiological preparation.

However, what happens when Americans who are interested in missions are repeatedly exposed to the broad Western media interest in images of wars and suffering in African countries like Uganda? It is most likely that if Americans know anything about Uganda, they know only Uganda's tragic moments. Continual exposure to Ugandans as hopeless cases shores up stereotype threat. The European colonization and imperialistic period was one of immense challenges along with other internal issues that impacted the people of Uganda. History shows that the ills that plagued Uganda had their deep roots in both the colonial and postcolonial era.[41] Some American evangelicals' perceptions of people in Uganda are as much a learned reality as it is for Christians in Uganda and their outlook of life in America. McCarthy writes,

> The highly unfavorable image of Africa, collectively projected by well-known commentators including Henry M. Stanley and Paul Belloni Du Chaillu as well as by obscure missionaries, tended to lend support to ideas of black inferiority held by while Americans. The view of Africa that became dominant, and which was often shared by diverse Americans, described it as a land of wild, exotic landscapes and fever-producing climates, intellectual back-wardens,

---

40. Schulzinger, *U. S. Diplomacy Since 1900*, 1.

41. Weinstein, *Inside Rebellion*, 63.

and economic retardation; a land whose native inhabitants were an "ignoble," morally depraved people devoid of modesty.[42]

America's history of race and ethnicity comes into focus due to further inquiry on the discriminatory attitudes and anti-African legacy. While the previous evidence of racially biased attitudes deserves to be placed in a dated and unfortunate epoch of America's past, anti-black beliefs are still ubiquitous. Hall shows,

> In one study, we randomly assigned white participants to associate words with either blacks or African-Americans. Specifically, they selected 10 terms out of a list of 75 (e.g., aggressive, ambitious) that they felt best described each group. The participants that evaluated blacks chose significantly more negative words than those who evaluated African-Americans. Notably, whites did not associate more negative words with "Whites" than with "Caucasians."[43]

The recent carnage of nine innocent African Christians by a white supremacist American during a bible study at the African Methodist Episcopal Church in Charleston, South Carolina, also lends more evidence to the ongoing black and white racial tensions in American life. A follow up question which this book will not sufficiently address is: How and to what extent does the above domestic racial social imagery influence American evangelical Christians who are eager to work in Uganda? Meanwhile, it is common to find a decent amount of Ugandan evangelicals who appear to have plainly absorbed the internalization of an identity of inferiority. This is usually in contrast to the favorable image of their well-endowed American Christian counterparts. Dowden describes the paradigm through which he was perceived while on a visit in Uganda:

> I was loved because I was white and rich, and from the rich world. I had come to bring its benefits to Africa, had I not? "So please Sir Richard, Master, Teacher, My Lord, Your Majesty." . . . To them I was someone who had come to help kill off old Africa and replace it with European ways. . . . They despised the old Africa and wanted to be Western.[44]

Thus, it is clear that there is need to discuss the impact of the assumptions that American evangelical Christians hold about Uganda Christians and

42. McCarthy, *Dark Continent*, 1369–70.

43. Hall, "Whites View the Term 'African-American' More Favorably."

44. Dowden, *Africa: Altered States*, 34.

conversely the assumptions Ugandan Christians possess about American Christians. In order to grasp contours of the above global church relationships, this book examines the social-historical perspective and how they continue to sharpen ecclesiastical and missiological relations globally. American Christians in evangelical contexts possesses certain worldviews about people's lives in Uganda. Such outlooks emerge from a historicity not apart from a Western missionary's evangelical background. According to Hastings,

> Early Christian missionary activity in Africa was both ethnocentric and iconoclastic in its attitudes toward Africans and their way of life. . . . Neither in the nineteenth nor in the early twentieth centuries did missionaries give much thought in advance to what they would find in Africa. What struck them, undoubtedly, was the darkness of the continent; its lack of religion and sound morals, its ignorance, its general pitiful condition made worse by the barbarity of the slave trade. Evangelization was seen as liberation from a state of absolute awfulness, and the picture of unredeemed Africa was often painted in colours as gruesome as possible, the better to encourage missionary zeal at home.[45]

Although the Western Christianization and colonization of Uganda and Africa were countered by uprisings and quests for independence, the postcolonial era is still burdened with assumptions and ignorance about intercultural interaction between Uganda and the United States. The desire to sojourn to Uganda on a mission to emancipate Africans can also be traced to the theological motivation of American Christians. It is also crucial to note that both the traditional and contemporary short- and long-term missionary international enterprise still enjoys a dominant market share in its missionary business model. There are no signs that the arrangement will change in the foreseeable future. As many Ugandan and American Christians continue to meet and interact with the aim of forming partnerships, their awareness and prevention of stereotype threats is to the advantage of positive interdependent partnerships.

45. Hastings, *Church and Mission*, 60.

Chapter 5

Fighting with the Lion

"Obwavu mpologama" – Poverty is a lion

A PHRASE IN LUGANDA, A LANGUAGE COMMONLY SPOKEN IN CEN-
TRAL UGANDA

The poor you will always have with you,
and you can help them whenever you want.

JESUS CHRIST (MARK 14:7)

Truly I tell you, whatever you did for one of the least of these brothers and
sisters of mine, you did for me.

JESUS CHRIST (MATT 25:40)

GOD'S LOVE AND CONCERN for the poor and people who have fallen on
hard times is well documented in the Old Testament as well as in the New
Testament. However, when it comes to the ministry of helping the poor,
stereotype threat is prevalent. When it comes to the economic state of some
of the poorest nations in Africa, Dambisa Moyo a global economist states
that "Africans are viewed as children, unable to develop on their own or
grow without being shown how or made to."[1] In keeping the self fulfilling
nature of stereotype threat, the "trouble with the [stereotype threat depen-
dency] model" is that the great commission suffers from great omissions.
Jesus, who is the originator of the great commission of sending his following

1. Moyo, *Dead Aid*, 32.

to herald the good news of his eternal love and forgiveness, detests the stigmatization of the poor. To be sure, I am not in favor of the contemporary missions frenzy of "go save the poor." It never works and in fact ends up perpetuating the child-like stereotypic worldview of the poor.

What really works is empathy for the poor and people willing to join the poor in their fight against poverty by helping one another with the relevant skills, information and approaches in a manner of "cooking the meal together" as a strategy of getting out of poverty together. At the risk of possibly playing into the stereotype of life in Africa as the drama of the fabulous act of *The Lion King*, let me pose a question. Did you know that I've fought with a lion? But how did it end? When I first saw *The Lion King* (my favorite musical ever) on Broadway in New York City where I used to live, I was fixated on the fight between Simba, the protagonist, and Scar, the villain. Both are lions, but which one of them was more frightening? All the while watching the lions on the hypnotizing stage, I also mentally drifted to my days of fighting with the lion. There is a phrase in Uganda that goes "obwavu mpologoma." The literal and direct translation of the phrase from Luganda into English is "abject poverty is a lion." We find lions in the jungle, at circuses, and on *The Lion King* stage. Yet there is also the metaphorical lion of abject poverty, which threatens what Paul Collier, an economist who taught at Harvard, directed the World Bank's research department, and is a professor at Oxford, has called people who live at the "bottom of the world economy."[2]

I am using the analogy of the lion as symbolism for abject poverty and its products of both misery and destitution. It might be helpful to notice that being poor might even carry a different meaning. For example, according to the Oxford dictionary, the term poor is defined as "lacking sufficient money to live at a standard considered comfortable or normal in a society."[3] I experienced both being poor and living in abject poverty as a teenager and in my early young adult days, plus the existentially excruciating pain from the brutal bites of abject poverty. The idea behind fighting the lion is also deliberate because even though I was faced with mountains of poverty and steep messages of helplessness, I never stopped fighting the good fight along with faithful friends who joined me by the mercies of God.

In Uganda, access to a quality education is the difference between opportunity and a flourishing future, and a hopeless existence. I remember

2. Collier, *Bottom Billion*, 60.

3. "Poor," *English Oxford Dictionary*. http://www.oxforddictionaries.com/us/definition/american_english/poor.

the first time my teacher sent me home from school, for lack of school fees, and told me not to return. I was in primary five. I was living in poverty and in a country that was still dealing with the after-effects of war, epidemics, and international policies of structural adjustment programs and how that trickles into the daily life of nations in Africa. My parents at the time were unable to pay for my school fees. I remember the shame and humiliation of being out of school. I needed less than $8 to safely stay in school. I sat by on the hillside near the classroom block with my paper and pencil and strained to hear the teacher from an open window in the distance. I remember another instance when I was sent home again from school for defaulting on school fees, curling up in a corner on the floor crying in the dark due to the inability to afford electricity, and begging God for an education.

From primary five through my secondary education, my family struggled to pay my school fees and I was out of school for weeks, months, and years. However, by the grace of God, over the course of my education journey and now career, my school fees were provided through a generous neighbor, friend, or family member. I am grateful to say that God not only provided my school fees to allow me to graduate with my high school diploma, but he enabled me to succeed in my university career to even recently earning a doctorate degree.

Definitions of poverty

Poverty is a complex and real fact of life around the world. When you desire to participate in God's global mission and especially in areas where the problem of abject poverty is prevalent, it's only reasonable that you know the issues before providing solutions. Have you ever wondered about how much a person needs to accumulate, to be considered a respectable participant in their society? It might seem like a strange question to ask in the twenty-first century, how various countries determine whether or not you live at, below, or above the poverty threshold, but you and I are categorized by such formulas all the time. I have respect and admiration for people who work hard and in due course earn profitable financial rewards for their labor. Indeed, "the worker deserves his wages."[4] At the same time, I am curious as to why the poor are surrounded by negative stereotypes. Of course, there are some people who unfortunately act and lead irresponsible

---

4. 1 Tim 5:18.

lives even when faced with economic hardship, and conversely some clear opportunity, but still abdicated self-leadership.

But how about the many who find themselves limited by other factors outside their control that contribute to their economic hardship against their will; for example, children caught in abject poverty. It has even become fashionable for many who claim to work on behalf of "the poor" to monetize the brand of the "least of these" and even profit from their effort in social entrepreneurship. Yet still, its the poor who get a bad rep. The poor are the product of the poverty industry within which fundraising is highly competitive in pursuing budget bottom lines. Dayo Olopade, in her book *The Bright Continent: Breaking Rules and Making Change in Modern Africa* provides an ideal example in her discussion of predatory so-called poverty alleviation schemes. Olopade, who holds a doctor of law degree from Yale Law School and earned her Master of Business Administration for Yale School of Management, mentions "the poorly reasoned development planning that has little use—or does actual harm."[5] It is proper at this point to clearly state that I am not naive about people's ability to manipulate the ministry of helping for their own interest. Indeed, it is even possible that some people who are faced with certain financial hardship might have gotten there due to reckless and irresponsible ways. Yet again, helping as a ministry service is not the problem.

Moreover, what hinders potentially helpful solutions in the ministry of helping are implicit bias that fuel negative stereotypes about the people in need of help and, the helpers' insistence on abject ignorance amid the possibility of accessing the necessary information. In this regard, Olopade's example about the adverse effects of abject ignorance exercised by people from the West through donating "stuff [Africans] don't want"[6] is timely. For instance, the US based company TOMS shoes has mastered the business of turning "stuff [Africans] don't want in the first place" into prescribed solutions for the challenges the poor face, which in turn gives TOMS abnormal profits.

Olopade writes,

> The company offers conscientious consumers the satisfaction of helping people while shopping. Their model donates one pair of shoes to poor communities around the world for every pair of shoes sold. Unfortunately, the model ignores the fact that plenty of poor people have shoes, both on their feet and . . . available for

5. Olopade, *Bright Continent*, 53.
6. Ibid.

local purchase. In the end, it exploits shoeless people as a brand differentiator. My first encounter with the for-profit corporation was at a tony "awareness"-raising event in Manhattan's meatpacking district, at which guests were urged to leave their shoes at the door. The barefoot party was intended to approximate the harm shoeless kids face everyday. Unknown to most revelers: the true tragedy of bare feet is not shoelessness, but poverty—the inability to afford shoes, or much else.[7]

Perhaps the better approximate experience would have been to have people leave their wallets in their shoes and spend the week without both. In Olopade's findings, you can begin to understand how people with various interests in the poverty alleviation industry start out with intentions purported to look great outwardly by helping those in need, all the while bending at some point to turn inwardly for personal gain. If most mission organization leaders aren't aware of the moral implications caused by their high commitment to the preservation of their interest, it's likely that the poor will always be a group to be used and not helped. This goes counter to the Apostle Paul's request to his colleagues in the helping ministry. As an admonishment he writes, "All they asked was that we should continue to remember the poor, the very thing I had been eager to do all along."[8]

The writer of many New Testament letters clearly valued the ministry of helping by partnering with people who have fallen on hard times. A major challenge in global missions, which has also been exacerbated by the media's obsessive globalization of human suffering, has to do with the negative stereotypes about the poor. Most NGOs have grown accustomed to defining and branding people faced with economic hardship as "beneficiaries." Such language is counterintuitive. I have met people who have ideas on how to improve their quality of life but all they lack is the investment. To me, most of these people are innovators and local leaders-in-the-making, with names and stories; they are not just "beneficiaries." Such a careless branding by development agencies is a strategy that works against many people faced with hardship because while some get help, there is a dehumanizing effect. What Sudipta Sen declares "a conscious creation, based on difference."[9]

During colonization, the Irish's experience as the "cultural other" and poor outer group was not pleasant. According to Takaki, "Even

7. Ibid., 53–54.
8. Gal 2:10.
9. Sen, *Distant Sovereignty,* 153.

their Christianity was said to be merely the exterior of strongly rooted paganism."[10] "The Irish were described as lazy, 'naturally' given to 'idleness' and unwilling to work for 'their own bread.'"[11] Takaki recounts how "the colonists complained that the Irish savages were not satisfied with the fruit of the natural unlabored earth."[12] Incidentally, the above claims are the same generalizations that follow the poor, which is the perception that even justifies some people's inclination not to be of assistance to people who are genuinely in need of a helping hand. But you must ask who exactly are the poor and what do they say about their experience of poverty? This is crucial because the perpetrators of stereotype threat in missions suffer from the inability to listen to the pain, fears, and hopes of the poor. This is due to the callused skins of their eardrums, which are tone deaf with their inability to hear the voices that already exist. There is already a voice and the poor tell their stories often better than their purported helpers can hear. While poverty is a vicious lion, the poverty industry as the hunter tends to mistake the poor for the hunt. A certain African proverbs puts it best: "Until the [hunt] tells [its] side of the story, the tale of the hunt will always glorify the hunter."

In efforts to set aside preconceived notions about the so-called "poor" for now, I am convinced that the suffering experienced by people living in poverty can provide an avenue through which you might be able to enter their story. I believe the poor's definitions of poverty matter in their ability to communicate their pains, fears, and hopes for improved life conditions. Below are some definitions of poverty by the poor around the world, which have been adapted from material from the World Bank and interactions with missionaries and aid workers.

> Don't ask me what poverty is because you have met it outside my house. Look at the house and count the number of holes. Look at my utensils and the clothes that I am wearing. Look at everything and write what you see. What you see is poverty. –a poor man, Kenya, 1997

> We know what you are asking us to do will not work, but we have to do it because we need the money. –Indonesian pastor, 2013

> Poverty is humiliation, the sense of being dependent on them, and of being forced to accept rudeness, insults, and indifference when we seek help. –Latvia, 1998

10. Takaki, *Different Mirror*, 26.
11. Ibid., 27.
12. Ibid.

Very little land of poor quality; every generation gets poorer. –Uganda, 1998

We may be poor in material things, but we are rich in the eyes of God. –Kenya, 1996

If you don't have money today, your disease will take you to your grave. –an old woman, Ghana, 1995

If I had got husband who has a salaried job. –Uganda, 1998

I'm old and I can't work, and therefore I am poor. Even my land is old and tired, so whatever little I manage to work does not give me enough harvest for me and my children. –Togo, 1996

Why are you taking a picture of us? What will happen with that picture? It will raise you money, but I need a blood pressure cuff for my job, and I have been asking for one for many years. –Haitian community health worker, 2010

Why is it when people like you [Christian aid workers] come, we tell you what we are doing but you don't listen. Instead, you tell us what you want us to do while we search for money for our poor. –Vietnamese doctor, 2009

Many definitions of poverty describe and quantify people who are poor based on relative income. This leads to the demarcation of an income threshold, and people whose income is below the threshold fall in the poverty bracket. For example, the US Census Bureau provides poverty thresholds by size of family and number of children, i.e., for two adults and two children the poverty income per capita is $15,391.[13] According to a Uganda Poverty Status Report from 2014:

> Poverty is used to refer to income poverty, unless otherwise stated. Income poverty in Uganda is measured using a consumption aggregate (consisting of food and non-food items, both purchased and consumed out of own production), which is considered the most reliable measure of permanent income.[14]

Income is central to poverty issues no matter what you might think. When a person is broke and hard of cash and can't afford the basic needs of life, they will worry and face distress for lack of financial resource. Even Jesus labored to comfort his listeners to such effect, saying,

13. Dalakar, "Poverty in the United States," 2.
14. "Poverty Status Report 2014," 6.

> Do not worry about your life, what you will eat or drink; or about your body, what you will wear. . . . Worry about clothes? See how the flowers of the field grow. They do not labor or spin. Yet I tell you that not even Solomon in all his splendor was dressed like one of these. If that is how God clothes the grass of the field, which is here today and tomorrow, is thrown [away], will not much more clothe you.[15]

Clearly, Jesus knew of the worries and stresses and pain and confusion and how vicious the lion of poverty threatens your life. However, be wary of people who try to talk anyone out of poverty through acts of bravery. Jesus says don't worry because he will provide. I have witnessed situations where missionaries with $8 in their pockets say to the poor, "Don't worry because Jesus will provide while I get myself a Starbucks mocha latte." This seems to be diametrically opposed to the great commission that is so glaringly irresponsible for followers of Jesus.

Income as a measure in and of itself might not be sufficient to measure and provide well-rounded comparisons in certain contexts, therefore allowing for further debate. Wilson and Ramphele put it succinctly when they write:

> Poverty is partly a matter of income and partly a matter of human dignity. It is one thing to have a very low income but to be treated with respect by your [neighbor]: it is quite another matter to have a very low income and to be harshly depreciated by more [high income] neighbors. Let us speak then of human impoverishment: low income plus harsh disrespect . . . To speak of impoverishment in this sense is to speak of human degradation so profound as to undermine any reasonable and decent standard of human life.[16]

In global missions, followers of Christ should seek alternative approaches in order to understand poverty from people who are affected by poverty. This will move missionaries past their fears and anxieties fostered by stereotypical conditioning. I believe that there is a need to look at direct understandings of deprivation as well. The lack of quality education, proper diet, housing, friendships, family support, some form of energy, and fuel are key indicators of the consequence of the lack of income. Looking at poverty in other ways can help you appreciate the barrier of seeing poverty as a material issue. When you connect with the issue of poverty at a deprivation level, it is possible to enter the human stories of people impacted by

15. Matt 6:25–34.

16. Wilson and Ramphele, *Uprooting Poverty*, 5.

poverty, thus your ability to empathize and to help where and when you can, is likely to improve instead of fall prey to the choice of ignoring and trivializing the real experience of not having basic needs. That is a world-view of privileged armchair practitioners who can afford to touch the poor with a ten-foot pole.

There has been and continues to be much debate about the nature of poverty, but one thing is clear: poverty is relative to the region, country, state, time, and village to which you are local. What I find fascinating is the ongoing absurdity among Western missionaries who have the luxury to start the debate amongst themselves about how their richness is poverty. For example, a missionary in Honduras wrote in a missions magazine reminding American short-term missionaries that they are poor too. Is this what global missions have come down to? In Uganda, you never find people sitting around bickering as to whether a wealthy person is poor.

Causes of poverty

Not all poverty is equal, since "the moderate, working, and the very poor"[17] experience poverty at different levels. Then there are the differing views on the causes of poverty. On one hand you have, "those who believe poverty continues as an issue because of failures in personal responsibility and those who believe the government is the answer to all these problems."[18] Why are some people poor? Is it because they want to be poor? Obviously not, since it is a basic human trait to desire, want, and need the basic and necessary resources in life. You can witness this quality in Solomon's prayer.

> Give me neither poverty nor riches; feed me with food convenient for me: lest I be full, and deny thee, and say "Who is the Lord?" or lest I be poor, and steal, and take the name of my God in vain.[19]

We are created with the desire for something and somebody. Nobody was created without basic needs for life. From Dr. Seuss' phrases out of a children's book titled *The Lorax*:

> Everybody wants a Thneed. . . . I'm being quite useful. This thing is a Thneed. A Thneed's a Fine-Something-That-All-People-Need! It's a shirt. It's a sock. It's a glove. It's a hat. But it has *other*

17. James, *Wealth of the Poor*, 11.
18. Ibid., 17.
19. Prov 30:8–9.

uses. Yes, far beyond that. You can use it for carpets. For pillows! For sheets! Or curtains! Or covers for bicycle seats![20]

In fact, for some people, the quest for stuff culminates to materialism, which is a transformational process and consequently delivers injustice to both the materialist and those around the materialist. When insatiable appetites for power, materialism, self-importance, and prosperity take over a person, people, group, or nation, there will be probable causes of violence, war, rape, plunder, and poverty. In the case of the European settlers, the "New World" and its vast opportunities that included natural resources, power, free labor, and dominion over the land were a win. Yet Douglas B. Bamforth also notes that they

> virtually always created the kinds of disruptive conditions which are likely to have triggered episodic crises within contacted indigenous societies, as a result of disease-induced depopulation, environmental degradation, altered the Native American's tribal structures, economic relations, intentional disruption of indigenous political relations, forced relocation of group and other factors.[21]

In numerous conversations I have had with some of my good friends, I have observed the struggle of trying to make sense of the pro and cons of colonialism. For some it's a new topic of interest, for others it's a familiar and trodden road. If you want to make sense of colonial history, I have found Chinua Achebe's definition succinct and impactful. Achebe, a Nigerian novelist, poet, and professor, writes, "Colonialism was essentially a denial of human worth and dignity."[22] Despite the fact that for some people, the analogical lion of abject poverty I introduced at the beginning of the chapter might at times override the human desire for a good life, people's desire for a better life still remains. No matter the levels of poverty, most of the people faced with abject poverty want to participate in the fight out of scarcity toward a better life. For those who are bent on the stigmatization of the poor, such an approach promotes victimhood, encourages the view of the poor as an outrage, and sees the indigent as a wretched victim. There are those who identify the state of being poor with the operating effect of unrighteousness and sin, while riches are viewed as articulate indications of God's blessings. To the contrary, Paul Tillich in his book *Theologian of*

20. Seuss, *Lorax*, 22.
21. Bamforth, *Indigenous People,* 111.
22. Achebe, *Education of a British-Protected Child,* 22.

the Boundaries clearly argues that sinfulness has everything to do with "the state of the estrangement of man and his world from God,"[23] rather than being economically broke.

Poverty is not solely caused by broken relationships, for broken relationships might play a small and complimentary part in the cause of poverty. Is it the case that wealthy people are rich because they have unbreakable relationships? Any tendencies toward the affirmation of such notions are famous for the propagation of the gospel of prosperity. The gospel of prosperity propagates an idea and logic that attributes one's accumulation of wealth and enjoyment of a healthy life, to his or her righteous relationships. So if resource based poverty is as a result of a broken relationship with God, then the accumulation of wealth is as a result of a good standing relationship with God? How do you verify that? There are numerous possibilities for the existence of poverty. Indeed, the relationships between certain factors of economic development, namely human resources, natural resources, capital formation, technological development, sociopolitical factors, and, I would add, spiritual factors, matter. Other voices argue for "the lack of some sort of work ethic and cultural traits that have allowed others to prosper."[24] But what should one make of the TOMS shoes case I presented in the middle of this chapter? What about the story of the mosquito net maker in Africa told by Dambisa Moyo? She narrates:

> There's a mosquito net maker in Africa. He manufactures around 500 nets a week. He employs ten people, who (as with many African countries) each have to support upwards of fifteen relatives. However hard they work, they can't make enough nets to combat the malaria-carrying mosquito. Enter a vociferous Hollywood movie star who rallies the masses, and goads Western governments to collect and send 100,000 mosquito nets to the afflicted region, at a cost of a million dollars. The nets arrive, the nets are distributed, and a "good" deed is done. With the market flooded with foreign nets, however, our mosquito net maker is promptly put out of business. His ten workers can no longer support their families too.[25]

You can't blanket people and groups as lazy just because there are a few people who might be up to no good. How about the impact of poverty on the biological and early childhood development of children? Emerging

23. Tillich, *Theologian of the Boundaries*, 188.

24. Acemoglu and Robinson, *Why Nations Fail*, 3.

25. Moyo, *Dead Aid*, 44.

evidence suggests that living in poverty may indeed alter how the brain grows, which may have implications for a child's life chances through adulthood. Neil Damron at the University of Wisconsin-Madison prepared a report that explains the following:

> Recent studies analyzing the MRI brain scans over the course of children's lives have shown that children from poor and near-poor households have significantly lower average overall frontal and parietal lobe volumes of gray matter than children from wealthier families.[26]

Additionally, Acemoglu and Robinson also insist on the fact that certain societies are poor precisely because they are ruled by failed leadership of a narrow group of elites who have organized society for their own benefit at the expense of the vast mass of people.[27]

Positive value that can come out of experiencing poverty

Can any good thing come out of experiencing poverty? For reiteration purposes, poverty and especially abject poverty is extremely harsh and can have long-term negative effects. Clearly, in no way, shape, or form am I an advocate of any possibility about any intrinsic good in abject poverty. Let's not glorify suffering from abject poverty. Moreover, I believe in people doing all the right things to make sure that their qualities of life reach a steady level of their desires. To be exact, right things like saving, investing, education, giving, servant leadership, praying, exercising, reflection and resting, et cetera. I also believe in rendering a helping hand to people who might have fallen on hard times instead of kicking them while they are down. During my tense struggles with abject poverty, I was often motivated to see the silver lining in situations including and especially those that looked like setbacks to the onlookers. I did not do it alone. The small and positive changes forward that I was encouraged and convicted to make came about because of faith in God and wise counsel. The values I learned like love, patience, hope, and perseverance went a long way. Here, I am reminded of Napoleon Hill, who said, "Every adversity, every failure, every heartache carries with it the seed of an equal or greater benefit."[28] Even more pro-

---

26. Damron, "Poverty Fact Sheet."
27. Acemoglu and Robinson, *Why Nations Fail*, 3.
28. Hill, as quoted in Chang, *Wisdom for the Soul*, 294.

found was the opportunity to trust and depend on ngth and provision in spite of painful uncertainty.

Dr. Scott Burns, who is a close friend of mine, recently relocated from his home country of Scotland to the United States and is a living model in overcoming life's adversities. Dr. Burns, with the support of his wife Monica, friends, family, church community, and ultimately God's mercies, overcame testicular cancer. He is on the pastoral team at Grace Chapel in Oregon where he delivered a moving homily titled "He Embraces Weakness." Weakness is a common attribution among the poor. Yet Dr. Burns' perspective about the upsides of weakness echoes the words of C. S. Lewis, "Hardship often prepares an ordinary person for an extraordinary destiny." Instead of giving in to the "get tough on the weak" mind-set, this unbiblical, irrational, missiological mind-set whose mission is self-preservation from ostensible "harm," let us embrace the opportunities to help. For this was Christ's attitude to the Apostle Paul in his time of weakness. Christ said, "My grace is sufficient for you, for my power is made perfect in weakness."[29] Paul responded by acknowledging the silver lining in his situation and you, too, can do likewise. "Therefore, I will boast all the more gladly about my weaknesses, so that Christ's power may rest on me. That is why, for Christ's sake, I delight in weaknesses, in insults, in hardships, in persecutions, in difficulties. For when I am weak, then I am strong."[30]

Yet, I also recall the perplexing impact the "sights" of poverty had on visiting short-term missionaries from America. When I was driving in the streets of Kampala with a car full of my friends who were on a short-term mission trip and visiting Uganda for the first time from the United States, I turned to ask how everyone was feeling given the impact of jet lag, and every one of my friends seemed to have been holding up just fine. However, a few seemed distressed and one of them finally piped up to ask a question that went as follows: "What isn't poverty here?" Almost everyone in the car responded in the affirmative to his inquiry. I wondered to myself, what about the sight of poverty in their view was bothering them? What really surprised my upper class evangelical American friends? Was it shock? Were they moved by empathy for the people? Was it a psychological pain that triggered fear, anxiety, and false guilt in their imagination of a perceived agony of the Uganda context they had only experienced for a day?

29. 2 Cor 12:9a.
30. Ibid.

For corrective purposes, not everyone in Uganda is poor and not everything is or looks like poverty. There are places like the slums and other sights that will show the impact of poverty for sure. On the hand other, there are places in Uganda with affluence. Over lunch, I gave my response to my missionary friends' sense of shock. I informed them I did not see poverty in some of the places they identified in Uganda. To me, our difference of perspective had to do with the realization of the effects of broader and glaring economic disparities, which exist between the Western world and a country like Uganda. I told my American missionary friends that missionaries from the Western world are some of the wealthiest people in poor countries. I further asked some of them to reflect a lot more on what implications the social identity of affluence means for Western missionaries. Just as negative stereotype threats negatively impact the poor, people perceived as having affluence can either experience a "lift," given a positive look toward their wealthy identity, or distress otherwise. You can witness the distress in Michelle's advice to fellow American missionaries. In a prominent Christian magazine article, Michelle, who was born in California, gave a short-term missionary from America the following a piece of advice. She wrote, "If at the end of your trip you say, 'I am so thankful for what I have, because they have so little.' You have missed the whole point. You're poor, too. But maybe you're hiding behind all your stuff." In this case, Michelle confronted the Western missionary's social identity of affluence and the stereotypic language that comes with it. However, Michelle herself missed the point. It is never a bad thing for someone to be thankful for what he or she has. Gratitude is good any time. Shaming a person into realizing that they, too, are "poor" or "broken," is callous. Also, what does that say about Michelle's view of the "poor"?

Like Michelle, another American missionary in his early thirties told me that the reason he and his wife wanted Americans to come to Uganda on social justice trips and "rough it out," was that he intended to "break them." He went to great lengths to force the short-term missionaries to do manual labor, sleep on shabby mats, become exposed to malaria-infected mosquitoes, and be crowded in a small room. Never mind that he and his wife had their home in an expensive mansion in Kampala. Is the condition of being poor some type of underclass category and torture chamber suitable for the belittling of the affluent? Is that a gospel-centric attitude? What have missions come to? My hope here is that you will see the silver lining and the opportunity to reflect more about your assumptions and attitudes regarding the conversation about serving the poor.

Chapter 6

Today It's Me; Tomorrow It's Someone Else

Never reduce your life to the event you are facing right now;
if you [do] you are not going to see what's ahead of you.
HOWARD THURMAN

Who is vulnerable to stereotype threat?

WHEN IT COMES TO stereotype threat in cross-cultural missions and partnerships, all parties are vulnerable. Situational factors that come to bear in the relationships of Ugandan and American Christians are likely to intensify predispositions to stereotype threat. Davies explains that negative stereotypes in cross-cultural missions that target a cultural or social identity provide the risk of being judged or treated in terms of those negative stereotypes and can evoke a disruptive state among stigmatized individuals.[1]

Group membership

It is possible that every member of a group, ethnicity, and community, is vulnerable to stereotype threat in certain ways and situations. People in Uganda by and large belong to tribal systems made up of "tribal and clan units [with their] own forms of . . . religious, social, political, economic, and cultural values of that community."[2] The presence of any salient social identity of Ugandans belonging to any of their ethnic group is prone to

1. Davies, Spencer, and Steele, "Clearing the Air," 276–87.
2. Tiberondwa, *Missionary Teachers as Agents of Colonialism*, 1.

stereotypes. Consequently, the presence of any confirmed stereotype that negatively targets any of the noticeable social identities of Ugandans belonging to any of their ethnic groups can impact their participation in global missions intercultural relationships. Stereotype threat affects diverse groups of people ranging from generalizations such as "Ugandans don't think" to "poor people are lazy" and "men are better at business than women," to "all white Americans are racist."[3] Frantz, Burnett, Ray, and Hart clarify that, "though white people may not perceive their group as stigmatized, situational pressure is sufficient to induce stereotype threat and that internalizing the negative stereotype is not required."[4] This is yet another point of emphasis on the need to attentively study the environmental contingencies. They may lead to the acknowledgment of systemic issues, as well as other particular related threats to one's identity. Stereotype threat is no respecter of persons or creed. Additionally, according to Davies, Spencer, and Steele, stereotypes communicate to stigmatized individuals the "accusations" that specifically devalue their group's social identity.

Ugandans and people from Africa in general, for example, are likely to be well aware that stereotypes accuse them of being intellectually inferior and "aggressive; and women are well aware that stereotypes accuse them of being emotional, bad at math, and lacking leadership aptitude."[5] The environment in which group membership will experience stereotype threat in missions is a crucial factor. For example, colonial missionary strategies are not alien to the United States of America. While discussing the conquest of Native Northern Americans, Woodley asserts:

> During the boarding school era, missions were administered from a position of power and superiority to the supposed unlearned savage. The tragic history of US governmental civilization policies, such as during the residential boarding school era, is something akin to active genocide. An argument can be made that the Indian boarding school project was more like ethnocide than genocide, but when calculating the end result it makes little difference whether indigenous lives or indigenous cultures were destroyed because the two are so intricately intertwined.[6]

---

3. Frantz et al., "Threat in the Computer," 1610.

4. Ibid., 1613.

5. Davies, Spencer, and Steele, "Clearing the Air," 276–87.

6. Woodley, "Mission and the Cultural Other," 458.

Such historical data mentioned in the excerpt above happened, but it also matters in assisting one to appreciate the structural complexities that surround the nature of stereotype threat in global missions. Despite the effort of the civil rights movement in the United States, First Nations People, African Americans, and other racial minorities still experience domestic racial tensions.[7] Stereotype threat is a force to be reckoned with and therefore while preparing American missionaries for intercultural interactions, it is necessary that key aspects of race, ethnicity, and people group relations become integrated in missions training.

However, as important as it is to provide prior education about potentially contentious cross-cultural issues in missions, it is important to underscore that people's vulnerability levels in missions are not dependent entirely on their cultural skills and giftedness. For example, a study conducted by New York University's department of applied psychology about the effect of stereotypes on women who possess a high ability to perform complex mathematics exercise notes

> that women at the very highest levels of math ability are held back by cultural images that portray their math abilities as inferior to men's. . . . Furthermore, we know that stereotype threat is not some artificial laboratory phenomenon. It has real consequences for women who have extremely high abilities and who aspire to be scientists. While [the] study doesn't prove that sex differences in math ability are not the root cause of the lack of women in math and science, it does prove that biology is far from the whole story.[8]

Even though all people groups are susceptible to stereotype threat, it should not go without emphasizing that certain people groups encounter more stereotypic behavior due to the ubiquity of marginalization that is accompanied by stereotypic suspense of lower grade abilities. Ugandans and Africans have been portrayed with certain stereotypic images for centuries. During the establishment and boom of Western colonial missions, Keim reports:

> Since the nineteenth century, the root cause of African's backwardness was considered to be their race. Most whites believed, for example, that Africans lacked philosophy because they lacked the biological capacity to produce it. Over time, blacks would evolve the ability to philosophize like whites, to create real art, and to rule

7. West, *Race Matters*, 122.
8. "Stereotype Threat Affects Women."

themselves, but until that moment, the best that could be done was for white men to accept the burden of control and care, as one might do for children. . . . Because Africans were presumed to represent a more primitive time, most Westerners, including most Americans, could easily accept African subjugation and overlook African contributions to history. The idea of African racial inferiority dominated Western thinking until at least the 1960s and still has some currency in American . . . society.[9]

Failure to consider the importance of group membership dynamics in global cross-cultural missions might conceal the experience of stereotype threat to the detriment of people's possible willingness to participate in cross-culture ministration.

Group identity

When practitioners in global missions negatively elevate the social and situational description of a stereotyped group, social identity stereotype threat becomes imminent. Oblivion to the effects of using negativity while trying to create friendship-based global missions partnerships, only serves to focus on already threatened identities. Christians seeking to work in cross-cultural settings can be well served by the realization that although almost anyone is susceptible to stereotype threat, unevenly targeting people with group identities that are customarily marginalized, are the ones that suffer most.

Inzlicht and Schmader reflect on the stigmatization of groups by pondering the particular meanings to situational cues in the lives of stigmatized individuals. They suggest that members of stigmatized social groups—by nature of their stigmatized status—have multiple concerns in the settings they encounter. Inzlicht and Schmader have also shown that stigmatized individuals who are unsure as to whether others will judge them according to their identity, or whether their stigma carries a burden that impinges on their existence. Indeed, stigma carries with it additional burdens besides that of being reduced to a stereotype; people wonder how their identity will matter for many social and personal outcomes.[10]

The importance of knowing about group identity salience while attempting to develop global church interdependent partnerships cannot be

9. Keim, *Mistaking Africa*, 181.
10. Inzlicht and Schmader, *Stereotype Threat*, 23.

further stressed. When negligence toward the risks associated with race and ethnic identity makes its way in missiological policies, intercultural conflict is evident. Goffman argues, "As suggested, we are likely to give no open recognition to what is discrediting of [people's identity] and while this work of careful disattention is being done, the situation can become tense, uncertain, and ambiguous for all participants, especially the stigmatized one."[11]

Another element of group identity to focus on during the formation of faithful friendships and interdependent partnerships in missions is in-group and out-group interactions. Missions groups seeking to work together in intercultural situations will at time encounter group identity related issues. Understanding the challenge of threats to our identity can help us work to solve identity-based discord. It is easier to mistreat, mistrust, and objectify someone with whom we do not identify. This is one of the reasons that in conflict one of the key communication strategies is naming the "other" in disparaging and stereotyped ways—indeed, it is one of the first levels of the escalation toward intractability.[12]

Stereotype

Stereotypes in and of themselves, when active, are sources of vulnerabilities to stereotype threats in missions and can threaten people involved in cross-cultural endeavors. It is noteworthy to realize that while participating in missions activities, missionaries are bound to encounter people of all walks of life who are targeted by stereotypes. Stereotypes in intercultural settings can be surprising and obvious. Both positive and particularly negative stereotypes can have intended and unintended consequences. Stereotypes are part of society's means of communication and they are difficult to recognize in cases where they are deeply rooted and accepted as part of a community's language.

However, Pinel's reflection is a helpful reminder that innocent chatter, the currency of ordinary social life, or a compliment ("You don't think like a woman"), the well-intentioned advice of psychologists, the news item, the joke, the cosmetics advertisement—none of these is what it is or what it was. Each reveals itself, depending on the circumstances in which it appears, as a threat, an insult, an affront, as a reminder, however subtle, that I belong to an inferior caste.[13] Pinel's statements call for a consciousness and

11. Goffman, *Stigma*, 41.

12. Remland et al., *Intercultural Communication*, 77.

13. Pinel, "Stigma Consciousness," 114.

manner of responsibility that is cognizant of people and their communities in a respectful and gentle way. Intercultural situations present the opportunity to learn about the benefits of ethnic diversity, and with a reduction of threats, people's ethnicity can be secure.

Ethnic identification

As a country, Uganda is made up of ethnically diverse tribes similar to the First Nations tribes in the United States. Most Ugandans highly identify with their tribal, cultural, and national domains. Stereotype threat can take advantage of their identification and thus jeopardize the possibility of forging cross-cultural and interethnic partnerships. Identification in and of one's self is not the problem and should not be scapegoated. It is important to be mindful of stereotype threat's role in people's "dis-identification"[14] and therefore disengagement, especially among highly motivated potential and actual colleagues in global church missions. According to Saad, Meyer, Dhindsa, and Zane, "As this threat persists, it may lead students to disidentify with academics and decrease participation in intellectual domains overall."[15]

Effects of stereotype threat in intercultural global missions

Missionaries from anywhere and everywhere will encounter stereotype threat in global missions partnerships. In a world where people from many cultures are meeting regularly, the consequences from every intercultural interaction vary from culture to culture. Albeit, there are general consequences associated with stereotype threat. Here, a close glance is directed at the frequently destructive implications of those stereotypic threats in formation of mutual partnerships between Ugandans and Americans. Steele, an expert in stereotype threat, sheds more light on the educational purpose behind stereotype threat awareness. According to Steele, the mission is to broaden our understanding of human functioning and to get people to pay attention, especially in identity-integrated situations. People are not only coping with the manifest tasks of the situation, but they are also busy

14. Ibid.

15. Saad et al., "Domain Identification," 162.

appraising threats and protecting themselves from the risk of being negatively judged and treated.[16]

Decreased participation

When people involved in cross-cultural contexts are under stereotype
threat, they experience low participatory and performance effects. In the
opening story of this book, it is obvious that among the conflicts of Dana,
Tim, and their Ugandan counterparts were diminishing levels of interest,
participation, and thus low performance. Deaux, Bikmen, Gilkes, Ventu-
neac, Joseph, Payne, and Steele note:

> When a stereotype is believed to be relevant to a domain of perfor-
> mance, it poses the threat that the person will be judged or treated
> in terms of the stereotype. The impact of that threat is reduced
> performance on domain-relevant tasks, an effect that has been
> consistently demonstrated in scores of studies across groups vary-
> ing in gender, ethnicity, and social class.[17]

Negative influences on people's performance can affect participation levels
as well. While a drop in performance and participation is true for certain
situations as is evidenced with the Ugandans' response in the interaction
with the American missionaries, there are other related retorts. During a
study of first generation non-American black West Indian immigrants living in America on Africa and stereotype threat, Walton and Cohen discov-
ered that the stereotype elicited another reaction. According to Walton and
Cohen, the immigrants experienced another effect called "stereotype lift,"
which is the performance boost caused by the awareness that an out-group
is negatively stereotyped. However, the effect also happens in the absence
of a denigrated out-group.[18]

Internal attributions for failure

Given that this book focuses on both the Ugandan and American nexus
of missions partnership formation, the effect of "internal attributions for
failure" in the wake of stereotype threat might be expressed differently.

16. Steele, *Whistling Vivaldi*, 213.
17. Deaux et al., "Becoming American," 386.
18. Walton and Cohen, "Stereotype Lift," 456–67.

Humans have a reputation of interpreting people's actions based on assumption. According to Winkler, people tend to form individual thoughts about the reasons for particular events, including the behavior of others and one's self.[19] A pertinent example is the comment from the Ugandan woman who attended Dana and Tim's discipleship sessions. She remarked, "They are mistreating us because we are Africans."

For Americans, it can be the proverbial consciousness of "I stick out like a sore thumb" while in an interethnic situation. Categorically, Americans and Ugandans have different approaches to attributions. The general cultural response for Ugandans tends to be informed by a "collective"[20] outlook, while in American culture, "individualism reigns supreme."[21] In the case of a shortcoming or failure, Ugandans tend to perceive the effects of a situation with a collective concern for the thoughts and feelings of others in the community. In the United States, an individual's perspective is most concerned with one's own attainment of happiness, thoughts, and actions.

Excuses and self-handicapping

The process of mobilizing people to attend cross-cultural events where stereotype threat exists can lead people to be suspicious of the nature of missions activities. Disinterest in the legitimacy of church programs, bible studies, discipleship, and evangelistic community functions are some of the symptoms of task discounting. Under threat, the assignments in an intercultural situation can be viewed as tricky. In Klein, Pohl, and Ndagijimana's study of immigrant Africans from East and Central Africa under stereotype threat, the results where consistent with task discounting. The African participants in the study proposed that they had too little time or information, were tired or distracted, and that the events did not suit their nationality.[22] For some individuals, self-handicapping creates a separation path from the possible threats in a given situation.

---

19. Winkler, *Contemporary Leadership*, 9.

20. Rarick et al., "Investigation of Ugandan Cultural Values," 1.

21. Elmer, *Cross-Cultural Conflict*, 25.

22. Ibid., 460.

Distancing and disengagement from the stereotyped group

Avoidance is a common behavior in society. In regard to stereotype threat in interethnic relationships between Americans and Ugandans, avoidance and distancing is a problematic sign. When people remove themselves from a situation where the love of God is supposed to be articulated, there is something hindering their ability to appreciate and identify with the missions activities linked to their social group. Such a scenario is counterintuitive to God's love, which is the core of the gospel message.

Distancing undetected as a conflict management strategy is not beneficial for anyone in any given mission context. Elmer notes, "The person who tries to manage conflict by avoiding it believes that differences are bad, they always cause hard feelings and broken relationships."[23] Distancing in the event of stereotype threat also presents itself through "identity bifurcation."[24] Here, a person under threat will "identify *selectively*—that is, disidentify with the aspects of one's in-group that are linked to disparagement in that domain, while continuing to identify with valued in-group characteristics that are not seen as linked to such disparagement."[25] There are more ideas concerning the struggle and difficulty that stereotype threat brings upon its targets in intercultural and interethnic missions. Pronin, Steele, and Ross explain that identity bifurcation is not a good strategy to endorse. Indeed, there is poignancy, and even injustice, in such adaptation. Acute or chronic stereotype threat either on an individual or collective basis is ill treatment of people with judgment that forces them to pay an unfair price of "fitting in."[26]

Disengagement as a coping strategy from a threatening context is also another form of distancing that comes to bear in missions' stereotypic environments. Schmader, Major, and Gramzow argue that disengagement and self-protective strategies are more likely to be evoked in evaluative situations that threaten a person's self-view.[27] Perhaps an individual's attempts to deploy disengagements may strategically enable one to remain in a discomforting environment.

Stereotype threat is operative in cross-cultural, interethnic, and intercultural missions. While historical stereotypic events and the current

---

23. Ibid., 36.

24. Pronin, Steele, and Ross, "Identity Bifurcation," 152.

25. Ibid.

26. Ibid.

27. Schmader, Major, and Gramzow, "Coping With Ethnic Stereotypes," 93–111.

avenues of education influence the American theological, ecclesiological, and missiological contours, they have also played their role in the minds and hearts of the Ugandan population. However, the unnecessary stress, anxiety, and disunity that infringe on the global church's ability to forge faith friendships and partnerships are identifiable. Some theologians, cross-cultural thinkers, intercultural educators, and missiologists, in attempts to raise awareness about the rocky nature of transcultural context, have documented their opinions, which are shared in the following chapter.

Chapter 7

Past and Collective Experiences
in Global Mission

We are not makers of history. We are made by history.

MARTIN LUTHER KING, JR.

FOR THREE CENTURIES NOW, the Christian missions and the missionary movement has undergone remarkable episodes around the world. This missionary movement has enjoyed immense expansion through the evangelization of people groups around the world. In fact, as part of the missionary enterprise, particularly on the continent of Africa, certain areas witnessed a level of impact. According to Woodberry, missionaries were catalytic in the spread of mass education, hospitals, mass printing of Bible translations into local languages, newspapers, voluntary organizations, and the codification of legal systems.[1]

The missionary invasion narrative in Uganda and Africa would not be balanced without the gains experienced by the missionaries as well as the unforgettable failures. In concert with other setbacks of the Western mission enterprise named in this book, Nelson further states, "A major weakness in mission theories was a failure to recognize just how much the societies missionaries were working in were being transformed by colonizing forces other than missionary efforts."[2] The roots of the Christian mission are far reaching in nature and continue to spread among numerous ethnic and cultural global communities. The global progress of the Christian

---

1. Woodberry, "Missionary Roots," 244–74.
2. Nelson, *Christian Missionizing*, 13.

gospel rooted in Jesus Christ has for decades been preached on the African continent, in Europe, America, Asia, and Latin America. Yet the epochs of the journey of global Christianity have not existed without controversies.

There are evident moments when particular cultures and civilizations positioned themselves in domination even with the Christian faith. For instance, Jenkins notes,

> Over the last five centuries, the story of Christianity has been inextricably bound up with that of Europe and European-derived civilizations overseas, above all in North America. Until recently, the overwhelming majority of Christians have lived in white nations allowing some to speak of "European Christian" civilization.[3]

Jenkins's thoughts in the quote above seek to elevate and nurture interest in the ongoing phenomenon of the movement of Christianity because of the kind of Christendom in Europe and particularly American mission evangelicalism as it concerns this book. In general, Western cultural evangelicalism as a by-product of Western Christendom has been presupposed to be the "Christian faith, which is seen as the so-called soul of Europe or the West. The essence of the idea is the assertion that Western civilization is Christian."[4] This notwithstanding, the narrative is that Christendom is considered an element of the past in present-day Europe and in certain parts of North America, with a relatively strong evangelical presence in the latter, and a regressive Christianity in the former. Consequently, Christianity's ability to shift and move to geographical locations around the globe seems to be a recurrence, even to the augmentation of demographical realities globally. Jenkins demonstrably writes,

> Christianity has in very recent times ceased to be a Euro-American religion and is becoming thoroughly global. In 1900, 83 percent of the world's Christians lived in Europe and North America. In 2050, 72 percent of Christians will live in Africa, Asia, and Latin America, and a sizable share of the remainder will have roots in one or more of those continents. In 1900, the overwhelming majority of Christians were non-Latino whites; in 2050, non-Latino whites will constitute only a small subset of Christians. If we imagine a typical Christian back in 1900, we might think of a German or an American; in 2050, we should rather turn to a Ugandan, a Brazilian, or a Filipino.[5]

3. Jenkins, *Next Christendom*, 1.

4. Carter, *Rethinking Christ and Culture*, 14.

5. Ibid., xi.

The scope of research that already exists concerning the connection of Christianity with African cultural identity and the western missionary enterprise is broad and there is need to provide a survey of the literature. The works in review touched on the historical evidence of how African Christians have participated in the wide impact of global Christianity. Part of the task at hand for the intellectuals featured in this section is to address and unhinge the African Christian identity from pervasive hooks of Western missiological paradigms of dominance as stated in the earlier section. The layout of the literature will showcase the books used in this work, by discussing pre-Western Christianity and its missionaries' presence in Africa, the colonial rule period and post-colonial time to date.

Along with Jenkins's data mentioned above, there is an allocation of emerging literature that describes the overdue awareness on how diverse and dynamic global Christianity is beyond its commonly prejudiced confinement to only Western civilization. With the life and ministry of Jesus Christ of Nazareth as the kick-starter of Christianity as a global movement in its Mediterranean context, the religion's relationship with other continents such as Europe, Asia Minor, and Latin America have been broadly represented in history with dim exposure to the African contribution. The following contributors identified in the accounts below and during the course of this book will serve to discuss the stereotypical complexity that have marred Christianity and missions in Africa. This section will attempt to supply a panoptic view of Christianity's interaction with African cultures through the particular literary perspective.

Kwame Bediako—African culture and identity

The African theologian Kwame Bediako in his book, *Theology and Identity: The Impact of Culture upon Christian Thought in the Second Century and in Modern Africa*, labors to clarify the relationship between the gospel and culture as it relates to Africa's religious context in the pre-colonial and modern era. In the interest of understanding Africa's stereotypical image, Bediako digs back into Christianity's historical contexts. Further, he illuminates on how "Christian self-identity, therefore, emerges as an essential ingredient of the whole process that results in clearly defined theological interests."[6] Bediako's work attempts to authenticate the salient sensibility of

---

6. Bediako, *Theology and Identity*, xv.

the unquestionable need for any theology "to deal always with culturally-rooted questions."[7]

Bediako's initial remarks seek to establish the cogency of the book's basic argument, which parallels modern African Christianity and Graeco-Roman Christianity of the second century in "correlation, particularly for a correct interpretation of modern African theology in the post-missionary era."[8] Based on the author's backdrop and methodological setting, the beginning part of the book assesses challenges of identity encountered by early Hellenistic Christians and the demanding questions their thinkers faced about spiritual, cultural, and intellectual life. According to Bediako, once this perspective is granted, it becomes clear that the historical development of the Christian religion during the early centuries was witness to more than the interaction of Graeco-Roman and Christian ideas. "The process of continuous translation of Christianity's sources aimed at giving the Graeco-Roman world an . . . understanding of their context . . . [and established] an authentic Christian identity within their culture, meaningful both for them and for the world as it was then known."[9]

Although Bediako's seminal work does not outright deploy the idea of stereotype threat theory, it is relevant for this book because it travels through the historical parallels mentioned above, looking forward while assuming a solely post-Western missionary era. The material also highlights and elevates the significance of identity in interethnic and global church missiological relationships. The author labors to discuss the shift from a strictly Western missions outlook because of the historical approach of "the image of Africa in the corporate European mind during 'the Great Century' of the Christian missionary advance,"[10] which still lingers today. Euro-American centric missions understandings can still be evidenced in "the lie to the supercilious but tacit assumption that religion and history in Africa date from the advent in that continent of the white man."[11]

Even with the deleterious implications of the previously mentioned stereotypical categorizations of Ugandans in the realm of the Christian religion and its missions and African life, it is crucial to point out that Western missionary activity is not the original source of this lamentable perception.

7. Ibid.

8. Ibid.

9. Ibid., 33.

10. Ibid., 226–27.

11. Ibid., 2.

The previously discussed Western negative outlook toward Africans pre-dates the Western missions enterprise. Bediako notes that the unfortunate attitudes, images, and negative stereotypes formed in the Western world during the mid-nineteenth century of the racial, social, spiritual, and cultural inferiority was heavily influence by the slave trade, which shaped negative European attitudes and stereotypes toward Africa.[12]

Furthermore, the author unravels the historical impact of the West's effort toward the Christianization of people in Africa during "the period of Christianity's third [and blossoming] opportunity in Africa"[13] when the foreign cultural Western practices of Christianity were definitively taught "as civilization."[14] The missionaries' lack of prior understanding and genuine exposure to the African cultural and religious ways of life served to embolden the processes of severing African adherents from their cultural and religious heritage toward Christianity.

Bediako's additional arguments point to the consequences of a crippling Western ethnocentric missiological approach. He notes, "By not allowing in the first place for the existence of a 'heathen' memory in the African Christian consciousness, the widespread European value-setting for the faith created a Church 'without a theology.'"[15] Bediako's works help bring to the open the theologically disadvantageous impact of the colonial missiological approach. Here, the stigmatized group is directly affected by a supposedly Western theological attitude of paternalism, which de facto renders the person associated with the stigmatized characterization through power trips, which also play out in a socioeconomic distribution of stigma. Bediako relevantly demonstrates how unchallenged theological ideas assumed to be appropriate for other local contexts can be hazardous to a people's Christian and social identities.

With the surge of Christianity in African nations like Uganda, and the geographically central posture it holds for partnership with American evangelism, it is necessary for any mission's interest to explore the presence of stereotype threat in the case of both parties. This is imperative because negative stereotypes and stigma threaten to decay desired relationships of mutuality in missions to the detriment of helpful cultural intermediaries that matter most to people in a given local context. Furthermore, it is crucial

12. Ibid., 226.
13. Ibid., 227.
14. Ibid., 225.
15. Ibid., 237.

to uphold the biblical interconnectedness of believers in Uganda and those from the United States. The eighteenth century influential philosopher Hegel's thoughts on the people of the African continent he portrayed as primitive provides an idyllic justification. Hegel asserts,

> The peculiarly African character is difficult to comprehend, for the very reason that in reference to it, we must quite give up the principle which naturally accompanies all our ideas—the category of Universality. In Negro life the characteristic point is the fact that consciousness has not yet attained to the realization of a substantial objective existence—as for example, God, or Law—in which the interest of man's volition is involved and in which he realizes his own being. This distinction between himself as an individual and the universality of his essential being, the African in the uniform, undeveloped oneness of his existence has not yet attained; so that the knowledge of an absolute Being, an Other and a Higher than his individual self, is entirely wanting.[16]

Negative stereotypes of Africans like the ones espoused by the Hegelian outlook subtly find residence in society and even influence the course of global church contexts for both short- and long-term missions. Even though Hegel's perspectives are perhaps a representation of his time compared to people in the twenty-first century's view of Uganda, his far-reaching influence around the world is undeniable. More of Hegel's attitudes capture the fearfulness with which negative stereotype threat operates, which in turn affects the perpetrators of stereotype threats. Working in an intercultural setting calls for a higher ability to listen, learn, and engage emotionally. However, the converse is possible when one takes into account Hegel's positions. Case in point, Hegel's notion is that people of African descent exhibit the natural man in his completely wild and untamed state, and he called for Westerners to lay aside all thought of reverence and morality—all that Westerners call feeling—if they were to rightly comprehend the African's experience.[17] In the Hegelian posture, there is nothing harmonious with humanity to be found in the type of African he characterized. Hegel corroborated his point of view by noting, "The copious and circumstantial accounts of Missionaries completely confirm this."[18]

16. Hegel, *Philosophy of History*, 93.

17. Ibid.

18. Ibid.

Unlike Hegel, Bediako seeks to articulate a counter-narrative of the stereotypical contemptuousness, through an analytical perspective of both a theological and historical salience. Bediako addresses the missionary movement as a wing of a benevolent Western endeavor "to elevate the condition of African peoples, which meant that they must not only be given Christianity but also a total western cultural package."[19]

Along with this ideology, were the brains of scholars working to disseminate racial theories that emerged to unfairly dominate the Western mind-set with the idea of most African cultures as inferior ones? According to Bediako, the task of classifying and theorizing on the religion of African societies fell not to those who were the first to have close human contact with African peoples in the African context, that is, Christian missionaries, but to [Westerners] who only had minimal contact with them and who were, "at the time they wrote, agnostics or atheists."[20]

In this category were some of the influential pioneers in the then new sciences of anthropology and comparative religion, both of which finally came into their own on the basis of Darwinian evolutionary assumptions.[21] Western theoreticians like John Lubbock, E. B. Tylor, and J. G. Frazer were products of the Christian civilization of their time, but the nature of their own religious convictions and confession remains problematic.[22] Neither were these writers particularly concerned with the distinctly religious and theological objectives of the missionary movement.[23]

Theirs was a quest for the origin of religion in the history of mankind, constructed on a strict evolutionary scheme of development from lower, simpler forms, to higher, more refined and complex levels of culture. Since they associated levels or stages of material culture with corresponding stages in mental and spiritual culture, lower material accomplishments of "primitive" people pointed naturally to equally backward levels of moral, religious, and intellectual development. Consequently, "fetishism" or the later, more enduring term "animism"[24] with its associated ideas was simply

---

19. Bediako, *Theology and Identity*, 227–28.
20. Ibid.
21. Ibid.
22. Ibid.
23. Ibid.
24. Ibid.

the religious counterpart to the general social and technical inferiority of uncivilized and savage peoples.[25]

Donald Lewis, 'Christianity Reborn'

Donald Lewis's *Christianity Reborn* presents a thorough look at the expansion of evangelical Protestantism throughout history. The essay collections are scholarly in nature and effectively navigate through the widely documented phenomenon of the spread of Christianity in the non-Western world, namely Africa, Asia, and Latin America.

The book begins with an introduction, which outlines the rest of the sections. The literature is organized in fives sections. Chapter 2, titled "Evangelical Identity, Power and Culture in the "Great" Nineteenth Century," in particular, reverberates with the themes pertinent in this book. In the essay, Mark A. Noll, discusses "the history of evangelical Christianity that takes the entire world as its domain, 'the nineteenth century' . . . stretching from 1792 to 1910."[26]

Noll's grasp of the key events in the history of missions like the World Missionary Conference of Edinburgh in 1910 is timely for this book. The Edinburgh gathering in 1910 featured unique elements of excitement and regrets in global missions. Andrew Walls writes,

> The World Missionary Conference, Edinburgh 1910, has passed into Christian legend. It was a landmark in the history of missions; the starting point of the modern theology of missions; the high point of the modern Western missionary movement and the point from which it declined; the launch-pad of the modern ecumenical movement; the point at which Christians first began to glimpse something of what a world church would be like.[27]

At the historical event in missiology named above, the discussion and concern for foreign missions to mean the non-Western cultural locations like Uganda took center stage. The enthusiastic style of language used to describe various regions for evangelistic interest beyond the Western hemisphere was "carrying the Gospel to all the Non-Christian World Area . . .

25. Ibid., 230.
26. Lewis, *Christianity Reborn*, 31.
27. Walls, *Cross-Cultural Process*, 53.

Africa,"[28] and also illustrates the irresistibility of the condescending attitude and negative stereotypical outlook that engulfed Western colonial missiology. Currently, it is also necessary to note that groups like the Lausanne Movement[29] continue to make progress away from such perspectives.

Brian Stanley, who is another essayist in Lewis's book, provides an in-depth analysis of the World Missionary Conference's links to some of the prevailing prejudicial views of Ugandan and African culture in missions. Stanley is the author of chapter 3, titled "Twentieth-Century World Christianity: A Perspective from the History of Missions." Stanley clearly states that the fulfillment of the prophetic view from Edinburgh, which was to carry the gospel to non-Western contexts, was based on and depended on the willingness of the Western churches to give foreign missions the central place.[30] A Western-dominated mission approach appears to be perennial and thus an accomplice to the construction of the wide spread of the stereotypical notions of places like Uganda being subordinate and weak. Stanley further explains that the strongest voice at "the conference was one of boundless optimism and unsullied confidence in the ideological and financial power of Western Christendom,"[31] which usually serves to embolden the transportation of stereotypic ways. The expansion of the Christian message was not free of the nationalistic grips of "European or American influence or control."[32] Consequently, according to Stanley, the Edinburgh meeting failed to recognize the extent to which the open door for missions that so excited its enthusiasm was indebted to the increasing impact of European Colonialism. Colonial governments were seen as a good thing for missions on account of their supposed respect for freedom, Christian morality, and law and order.[33]

Too often, ignorance and hubris are part and parcel of the blind spots that hinder cross-cultural, interethnic, and transnational partnership in missions. While some Western missionaries like Sir Wilberforce opposed slavery, Lewis, Noll, and Stanley highlight complicities of Western missionaries and the materialization of unfair images of Africans, both in colonial and present times.

28. Grillo and Tonkiss, "World Missionary Conference Records," 7.

29. "Lausanne Covenant."

30. Lewis, *Christianity Reborn*, 52.

31. Ibid., 54.

32. Ibid., 57.

33. Ibid., 59.

Along with such nearsightedness came the handicap tendencies for the mind-set represented at Edinburgh to think predominately in ways that benefited Western evangelistic methods, "and only rarely in terms of incentives or disincentives for non-Westerners."[34] As is the focus of this book, derogatory and stereotypical attitudes in missions were rampant in the past. Stanley reports of an incident in which a new missionary of a major denomination who left for East Africa in 1861 was told repeatedly by his friends that he was wasting his time on those who lacked the moral and intellectual capacity to respond to the gospel.[35] Even though such claims are not valid, they are examples of the negative views about Ugandans in certain situations that involves intercultural missions between Ugandans and Americans.

Curtis Keim, 'Mistaking Africa'

Curtis Keim, the author of the book *Mistaking Africa,* avails a helpful understanding of African stereotypes and history. In chapter 1, Keim discusses how most Americans know little about African countries like Uganda. They might have studied Africa for a few weeks in school, glanced occasionally at newsletters,[36] or sat through social media and marketing sound bite videos used for fundraising purposes. Keim's work tackles numerous understandings of the African people and culture through the historical background of the existing stereotypes.

The issues and myths he exposes and discusses, plus the ethical and speculative ideas laid out in the book, are sufficiently salient for any inquiry into matters concerning the miscategorization of African culture and its complex history by Americans. Keim divides the sections of the book in four parts. The first part starts the book with the topics of "changing our mind about Africa." In the beginning section, the author insists that an African country like Uganda and the people of the African continent, "are simply a marginal part of American consciousness. Africa [Uganda] is, however, very much a part of the American subconscious. Ironically, although we [Americans] know little about Africa, [Americans] carry strong mental images of the continent."[37] Keim's perspective is helpful because it

---

34. Ibid.

35. Ibid.

36. Keim, *Mistaking Africa*, 1–5.

37. Ibid., 3.

highlights the need to take seriously the challenges that can be imposed on intercultural partnerships, even by stereotypic ignorance.

Furthermore, the analysis in the earlier part of the book ably addresses the limitations and challenges presented by the human inability of most Americans and—in this study's case—American evangelicals' willingness "to become experts on more than a couple of subjects" related to non-American cultures. The lack of interest to respectfully engage with other cultures and their communities has more than one source. In regard to the proper appropriation and misappropriation of stereotypes, Keim shows that the ideas that swim in the American evangelical psyche are a part of human existence and emerge from a cultural context. He writes,

> We also stereotype because it is virtually impossible to know everything that is going on in reality, and therefore we are bound to base our judgments on partial information. Like the proverbial blind men and the elephant, we each take our separate, limited experiences and extrapolate to make sense of the whole. Moreover, we often use ideas provided by our culture instead of investigating things for ourselves. If our culture has a pre-made picture of reality for us, we are likely to accept it. One way to think about this is to invert the notion "seeing is believing," making it "believing is seeing." Once we "know" something through our culture, we tend to fit new information into the old categories rather than change the system of categorization.[38]

The author's assessment of the American cultural landscape plays a part in the formation of who Africans are to the understanding of most Americans. Moreover, America's historicity also seems complicit in how it shapes and helps to provide certain persistent stereotypical outlooks of Africans as savage, intellectually weak, and inferior. Keim discusses the period during much of American history where a large majority of Americans considered racism and exploitation of Africa acceptable.

Although the United States never ruled colonies in Africa, Americans' historical participation in both the trans-Atlantic slave trade and a segregation system remains part of the narrative. Consequently, America's profiteering from the businesses of the trans-Atlantic slave trade exploitatively promoted the notions of people of African decent as inferiors. Essentially, there has been an extended practice for hundreds of years of constructing

---

38. Ibid., 7.

Africa as inferior.[39] However, Keim is intentional to acknowledge the progress made in America's racial domestic front. Racial tensions are still a factor, "but most derogatory images of Africa can no longer appear in public spaces."[40] However, these perspectives continue due to people's ability to learn stereotypes "in the more private aspects of our lives, from family and friends, and often through jokes or offhand comments."[41]

The second chapter, called "How We learn," explains how the misinformation and myths about Ugandans and Africans in general became a regular thought in the minds of most people in America. The prevalence of the historical images of life and existence in Africa are proliferated through the authorship of people who hardly experienced African culture. Biased print media outlets through their newspapers, the movie industry, and lopsided history books all contributed to the persistence of the poor understanding of the ways of life on the African continent. Keim notes,

> And the stories tend to be of two kinds, "trouble in Africa" and "curiosities from Africa." The "trouble in Africa" reporting usually follows a pattern. At any given time, only a handful of American reporters cover Africa south of the Sahara, a region containing a population more than twice as large as that of the United States.[42]

One of the prominent journalists in Uganda relayed his dissatisfaction with the manner in which a country like Uganda, its cultural contours and global geographical locus, are portrayed in the Western media. Oyango argues that a nation like Uganda is like other countries in the world that struggle with highs and lows. The patronizing representations one witnesses today are as bad as the condescending work of the past.[43]

Keim is mindful to discuss the progress that has been made in certain cases by the media. Indeed, it is possible to produce impartial news, images, and perspectives about an African country like Uganda. The author names journals like *The New Yorker*, *The Atlantic Monthly*, *Current History*, *Discover*, and *Vanity Fair*,[44] as examples of groups that exemplify some progress in the way images and stories from Africa are showcased. However, even with the reasonable attempts to improve the way the African

39. Ibid.
40. Ibid., 8.
41. Ibid.
42. Ibid., 18.
43. Ibid., 20.
44. Ibid.

continent has been depicted, there is still more to be desired. The negative news from the West about Africa still outweighs the positive. Newsletters from missionaries as sources of information about their work in certain African countries like Uganda need to upgrade from a lopsided approach of storytelling to one that is balanced.

Part two of the book introduces the notion of evolutionism and how the primitive idea of "Darkest Africa"[45] came to permeate and help form the viewpoint of most Americans about Africa. Henry Morton Stanley and Theodore Roosevelt are named as major American public and historical characters mentioned in the book as contributors to the derogatory and stereotypical attitudes.[46] Both were involved in various forms of news reporting: Stanley as a journalist and Roosevelt as an author of books about his escapades in Africa.

Tribes and the tribal reality in Africa are often misunderstood, and while some American missionaries are familiar with tribal definitions, others still the tribe with permittivity.[47] The genocide that happened in Rwanda is usually cited as an example of people in Africa who live in tribes and so the "tribal conflicts" in certain parts of the African continent are commonly mistaken for tribal wars. Such stereotypical outlooks are limited since there are more elements to tribal life, like traditional arts, storytelling, and cultural dances, than the assumption of wars. Keim cautions American evangelicals to be careful, however, not to assume that Africa's idea of tribe is the same as [theirs]."[48] Keim's work is relevant for this day and age of information technology and social media, which most of the people in Africa, even people who belong to tribes, have ready access to, particularly through cell phones.

Kwame Bediako, 'Christianity in Africa'

Bediako's book *Christianity in Africa: The Renewal of a Non-Western Religion* is structured in three parts and fully laden with historical case studies. Part one, "Christianity in African Life: Some Concerns and Signs of Hope," is concerned with the narration of past theological figures in Africa who demonstrated the intellectual fortitude to question the fittingness of the

45. Ibid., 47.
46. Ibid.
47. Ibid., 119.
48. Ibid., 199.

African existence and Western Christianity. In chapter 1, the author introduces the topic with the chapter title, "Is Christianity Suited to the African?" The author clarifies that this portion of the book observes a particular intellectual perception of the problem of African identity, which has it roots in the history of the contact of African people with the West.

While there were almost five centuries of near-regular contact, the problem with which we are concerned came to a head in the nineteenth century, when increasing Western cultural and political penetration and dominance in Africa coincided with an equally massive Western missionary enterprise. It is the African reactions to that cumulative Western impact on African life and on African self-identity that have shaped and conditioned the twentieth-century perception of the problem.[49]

Bediako discusses the impact of a historical African statesman named Edward Blyden, who was also "an ordained . . . churchman."[50] Blyden championed "the question of identity"[51] and influenced the dialogue about African identity in the midst of the expansion of the Western missionary enterprise. Bediako also quotes Blyden's concerns regarding the treatment with which Africans were widely viewed as people of a low-grade race by Western Christian nations, which was the amazing dissimilitude and disproportion between the original idea of Christianity, as expressed by Christ, and the practices of it by his professed followers.[52]

Furthermore, another icon mentioned by Bediako in chapter 2, under the subject of African identity, is Osofo Okiomfo Kwabena Damuah, who maintained that the imminent problem at the core of "the meaning of being African,"[53] was strongly associated with the propagation of Christianity as "Western culture"[54] and its links "to the colonial structure of Christianity's relationship with African societies."[55] The second part of the book details "Christianity as a Non-Western Religion: Issues Arising in a Post-Missionary Setting." Here, Bediako argues for Africa's primal religions as valid possessors of divine elements.

49. Bediako, *Christianity in Africa*, 5.

50. Ibid., 6.

51. Ibid.

52. Ibid., 13.

53. Ibid., 25.

54. Ibid., 27.

55. Ibid.

Part three examines the opportunities of African Christianity in the twenty-first century, which entails the destigmatization of culture in missions, the need to avoid the denigration of Africa's primal religious intermediary expressions, and an awakening to the role of the continent's vast political and economic complexities. However, the author's crucial argument of a "post-missionary setting" still leaves more to be desired since the presence of short-term missionaries continues to proliferate in Uganda, thus the quest of this book. The proceeding chapters in Part Three, "Into the Twenty-first Century—Africa as a Christian Continent: The Prospects and Challenges," touches on relevant themes applicable to this study. In chapter 13, "The Making of Africa: The Surprise Story of the Modern Missionary Movement," Bediako reviews old events that led to the understanding and leading of people of African decent as "primitive and savage." Bediako narrates,

> For towards the end of the slave trade era, in the late eighteenth century, when European humanitarianism coincided with the awakening of missionary concern, both humanitarians and their opponents were agreed on the image Africans: Africans were not only "savage" and "barbarous," they were also in "the very depths of ignorant [way of life]."[56]

Duane Elmer, 'Cross-Cultural Conflict'

Cross-cultural communication can be a challenge for people in both their local and global context. Duane Elmer's book, *Cross-Cultural Conflict: Building Relationships for Effective Ministry,* ushers its reader through several conflict scenarios. The book is structured in three parts. Part One, "Understanding Conflict and Culture" includes chapter 1, titled, "The Amazing Contours of Conflict." Elmer, who is a former American missionary to South Africa, admits his tendencies to having an "egocentric perspective . . . [and to] simply assume . . . superiority."[57]

Elmer's confession about his encounters and formerly held attitudes about black African people while serving as a missionary in Africa are telling. He writes, "During my early years in Africa . . . I began to conclude that

56. Ibid., 195.
57. Elmer, *Cross-Cultural Conflict*, 13.

black people were at best highly unreliable."[58] However, Elmer acknowledged the real problem at hand to be "the virus that resides in all of us . . . called prejudice." Beyond mere misunderstandings coupled with the willingness to learn and acquire a cultural framework necessary for the navigation of cultural challenges, Elmer demonstrated positive progress. Elmer's inclusion of "biblical insights"[59] to intercultural and interracial encounters is helpful in providing biblical underpinnings for cross-cultural relationships between Ugandans and American short-term and long-term missionaries. He identifies the problem of prejudgment, "racism,"[60] as "sin"[61] according to the Bible.

In chapter 2, "Cultural Diversity Was God's Idea (And So Was Unity)," Elmer begins with an assertion that "it was God who authored human diversity."[62] In fact, Elmer adds, "God looked around, saw a vast array of diversity in all he had created and declared it 'very good' (Gen 1:31)."[63] However, with the impact of sin and globalization's reach in both the local and global context one will, "experience cultural differences that have the potential to become cultural conflict."[64] Are most cross-cultural conflicts intentional? The author believes that cultural misunderstanding and

> conflicts resulting in brokenness are caused neither by core theological values being threatened nor by overt sin. Most conflicts that disrupt our lives grow out of innocent misunderstandings, unmet expectations, failure to get all the facts, or minor irritations that fester and become problems.[65]

Elmer's assessments of the challenges in intercultural and interethnic situations are beneficial for global church partnerships. Parts two and three are about subject matters of cultural diversity and conflict resolution, and their implication for the gospel message. The use and distribution of power in missions is another factor the author tackles ably. Both short- and long-term missionaries plus non-Western church and Christian organization leaders who receive financial support from the United States generally tend to have better standards of living than the average nationals. Regardless of

58. Ibid., 17.
59. Ibid.
60. Ibid., 18.
61. Ibid.
62. Ibid., 23.
63. Ibid.
64. Ibid., 17.
65. Ibid., 24.

how popular it is to talk about human empowerment, Elmer states that, "Whether Westerners or Two-Thirds World peoples, find it very difficult to give up power. Power is a great seducer; it leads us into illusions about our centrality to the work of God."[66]

Conclusion

Unlike the current ambivalent options people have about the Western missionary enterprise in Uganda and other African countries, excitement and participation in various forms of missions continues to grow in the twenty-first century. Ugandan missionaries are also enthusiastic about involvement in missions activities of a predominately local or country presence but not in the highly commercialized and internationalized Western missions manner. To that extent, the idea of missions prevails, but the sending organizations need to rethink the assumptions that tend to inform their preparatory processes. According to Woodley,

> Modern mission has taken good people with good intentions, who are ready to sacrifice much of their own worldly comforts, and inserted them into a system that most often results in missional hegemony. Power over others may appear via gender, race, ethnicity, or class status but it must depend on and be sustained by the very system which Jesus gave us a direct warning to avoid, namely, lording over others.[67]

What can be done? There are numerous and credible bodies of literature addressing cross-cultural communication, yet a dearth exists in the absence of a stereotype threat theory framework. Cross-cultural missiology literature, with the exception of a few, tends to generally focus on treating "win-lose"[68] strategies during the preparation of short-term and long-term missionaries destined for Uganda's cultural landscape. Other global missions training efforts use piecemeal methodologies, while certain groups rely heavily on Western psychometric curriculums as universally archetypal tools of acquiring intercultural intelligence. Such methods are at risk of failing to address threatening acceptances of missions and thus setting up missionaries for self-preservation and the glorification of heroism.

66. Ibid., 155.

67. Woodley, "Mission and the Cultural Other," 457.

68. Elmer, *Cross-Cultural Conflict*, 34.

Additionally, Elmer writes that missionaries who adopt a win-lose approach view every situation as right or wrong with a very small "gray" area, and tend not to be very flexible or willing to understand various global perspectives.[69] Similarly, non-Western cultural contexts with multiplicities of ethnic backgrounds are viewed from a fear-based outlook and thus missionaries are propped up to react toward the hot culture with subversive spiritualities. For example, missionaries display traits like "spiritual one-upmanship—say, [a power treat to] imply that God is on their [cultural] side"[70] against the "other." However, there are other processes from which people involved in global missions can be equipped to navigate through the fears that bedevil the domain of interculturality. This book uniquely extends consideration of "extra pressures that can affect the overall well-being and identities" involved in forging intercultural and bicultural global missions relationships between Ugandans and Americans.[71]

69. Ibid.

70. Ibid., 35.

71. Steele, "Stereotyping and Its Threat Are Real," 53.

Chapter 8

The Circle of Helping of 'Do Gooders'

Do not get weary in doing good.

SAINT PAUL

The helper is the helped and the helped is the helper.

MICHAEL BADRIAKI

Your constructs can cage you in, and then life does not go as well as it might otherwise.

BRIAN R. LITTLE (*ME, MYSELF, AND US*)

UP UNTIL THIS POINT in the book, I have discussed the tensions between helping or not helping and the significance of valuing the opportunity to help out somebody in need respectfully. I have introduced the presence of stereotype threat's impact in global missions and its negative effects on both the helper's identity and the one who receives help. Everyone at some point in this world needs some kind of help to cope with certain situations. I believe that people experience the circle of helping where on the one hand you are the helper, and then on the other hand you also become the helped. But in the following pages, I would like to zero in on an identified section of young people who I frequently meet at airports. You might have noticed them too. They usually huddle in groups and circles of teens and twenty-somethings at various gates before boarding the airplane, all geared up for the adventure in missions of helping the poor. Is there more to these groups than the stereotypic short-term missionizers with colorful T-shirts, tie-dyed hippie attire, REI clothing, and Teva sandals (or as we used to term this certain appearance: missionary clothes)? Are these mostly unprofessional and some professional missions helpers self-made and independently self-sufficient? You see, at times, both short- and long-term missionaries from wealthy nations seem to have it all together. An onlooker from the majority world could easy get lost in the impression that they are completely self-made. Bob Strauss, an American political figure and diplomat said, "Every politician wants every voter to believe he was born in a log cabin he built himself." But, as Strauss then admitted, "It ain't so."

Someone once said, "We stand on the shoulders of past giants." The renowned poet Maya Angelou wrote, "I come as One, I stand as Ten Thousand." You've benefited in some shape or form from some sort of assistance, an admission some nonetheless find hard to acknowledge. For many who value a sense of ragged mad determination to be self made, the tendency to think they don't need help is appealing. Yet when you take a closer look at your life's time line, you will see that as much as you've helped someone, you've been helped too. Even entrepreneurs borrow capital from the people who have suspended instant gratification. Capital is a form of help investors render to promising entrepreneurs by availing capital for investment, although for profit.

Stereotype threat presents itself in churches and global missions in many ways, as discussed in previous chapters, and derails people's performance in the helping ministry. How about stereotype threat and its manifestation in church leadership and missions strategies? Are your church's mission strategies promoting a missiological approach of helping that works? It is common to meet people who are interested in and at times enamored by the idea of missions. While some people encounter a sense of reward, although few in number, I am consistently amazed at the levels of disillusionments most short-termers and long-termers express with the messiness in missions they have encountered both in their home churches and the missions efforts their churches "do" in overseas missions. I know this first-hand because I spend a reasonable amount of time counseling and consulting with various groups, mostly in providing analysis on what went wrong and what can be done about it. I would like to mention some examples, but for the purpose of confidentiality, let me draw on Pastor Fred's story, which he has already published. Consider the pastor of a church in Midland, Texas, told by Pastor Fred R. Lybrand in his book, *About Life and*

Uganda: Insights from a Short-Term Pilgrim. When Pastor Lybrand and his leadership team asked that question, "What do you do with missions?", there was an underlying problem. Pastor Lybrand writes,

> We had noticed a trend for many years, and with the obvious needs of so many on a day-in-day-out basis, it was easy, even simple, to ignore the problem. The problem itself was that whenever one of our missionaries came to speak during a service or special event, people would scatter. Listening to a missionary to our average member was like playing Big Band swing music to the average American teen. Just the thought was enough to cause the ashen response of an anxiety attack. Why would missions, a well-known and important work for any "Bible-believing" church, keep people away? . . . In thinking about this issue, fortunately, it never crossed our minds to blame the members of the Church.
>
> Leadership often seeks to blame the members (just as the members try to blame the leaders), but a basic principle we've tried to follow is that the Church goes where the leaders take it. I had an even more personal reason not to blame the members. *I felt the same way.* Many missionaries made me want to scream! "Ooh," they'd say. "The work is so wonderful. See my pictures. God has really blessed us." And they'd drone on with tiresome stories of lands far away and tales that weren't intriguing or particularly impressive either. It seemed so far away from my life and the burdens and challenges I face daily. The challenges I face, as a "minister of the gospel" in America seemed ignored by most of my encounters with missionaries. They seemed to just skip over the difficulties we face in our own nation, and in our own churches; causing such a disconnection that it felt like watching a sci-fi flick about an other-than-here world. Of course, chances are they felt the exact same way. On top all of this, most missionaries I'd met left me feeling that laboring for Christ in America was less noble than laboring abroad; not to mention their freedom to criticize the American Church for being too fat, lukewarm, self-centered, lazy, psychological, etc.[1]

Again, the messiness of missions isn't all there is about missions, and some people have gained from their escapades. Yet it is obvious that stereotype threat is at play even in some of the informal helping relationships between the pastor, church leadership, the congregation, and the missionaries they support. You might have a totally different outlook than Pastor Lybrand, yet still, it's important for you to know that other Christians also

---

1. Lybrand, *About Life*, 6–7.

battle stereotype threat in missions. For those who find themselves turned off by your church's inability to provide in-depth preparatory training for both the short-term and long-term missionaries, what is the solution to such a predicament? Or you just might be wondering what to do with this messy thing called missions, wondering where to effectively start?

The act and art of helping is part and parcel of global missions. Jesus himself promised his disciples that he would make sure they got help. His promise was, "I will ask the Father, and he will give you another advocate to help you and be with you forever."[2] Jesus was a remarkable helper, full of comfort, mercy, healing, empathy, servant leadership, and justice. Humanity needs help and it is no wonder that the human race yearns for help, recognition, love, and peace as part of human survival. Paul encourages followers of Christ to keep on participating in kind demonstrations of both spiritual and social responsibilities. He writes, "Let us not become weary in doing good, for at the proper time we will reap a harvest if we do not give up."[3] This paints a clear picture that followers of Christ are agents of both spiritual and public kindness and love. They are the mouth, hands, foot, and "the body of Christ, and each one of [Christ's followers] is a part of it."[4]

The church in its local and global setting plays a critical and solemn role in this world, as Christ made visible. Christian acts of helping and charity are transporters and windows into the character of the global body of Christ and his saving life. Followers of Christ in their unity and global church diversity are then called to be instruments of peace. It was Saint Francis who prayed, "Make Me an Instrument of Your Peace." Even as I write to provide an alternative perspective that is contrary to what might seem obvious, I am sensitive toward the need for an awakened sense of solidarity. In an effort to rekindle and refresh a conversation about the characteristics necessary in your development in the ministry of helping and the navigation of stereotypic situations, below are essential stepping blocks.

Dear millennials, your ID matters in the helping vocation

Who are you? In my interaction with my students in class and on the various college campuses where I have taught as a guest lecturer, I have encountered statements of inquiry that cut to the issue of identity. Students

2. John 14:16.

3. Gal 6:9.

4. 1 Cor 12:27.

are intentionally and unintentionally on the equivalent of a Eurail pass in seeking to understand who they are and what they want to do in life. The lack of identity awareness can be unnerving for many people.

When you enter most hospitals, you not only see patients, but most certainly you also see medical helping professionals dressed in the standard dress code of a uniform and identity. The white coat and the scrubs are symbols of the profession and even social identity, but does that mean that a medical professional knows who he or she is? What you wear isn't the sole indicator of your profession. For a person can be an imposter, and wearing a white coat or scrubs, doesn't necessarily make you effective at work and guarantees that you have a grasp of who you are. How about the janitor; do you think all his or her worth is and can be reduced to what he or she does? You should learn to examine the presumptuous embodiment of perfection and intention. For example, anyone can wear a white lab coat but does that make him or her a physician? Wouldn't you want to know more about your "good intentions and passion for making an impact" by pondering of possible effects your actions might have on your neighbor, both locally and globally? How about the possibility that your identity issues might have a bearing on your intentions, which also embody what you value? Although these questions require time to arrive at answers I can scarcely provide here, how you think about your identity matters in life. Already, what comes to mind is a conversation I had with my friend Peter about his desire to help in intercultural settings both locally and globally, which I will elaborate in the pages ahead.

Threats to identity in the age of millennials

In the meantime, here I will discuss the salient idea of identity as it pertains to my experience with millennials and the fact that who they (millennials) think they are influences the choices and decisions they make. Who are millennials? They are a section of young people who are announced to be world changers. According to a Brookings survey conducted by Singer, Messera, and Orino on foreign policy:

> The millennials are the generational cohort born from roughly 1980 to 2005, in an "echo" of the Boomer generation. But as with other generations, it's not the exact date of birth that matters as much as their mind-set and transformative experiences. The other

names that the millennials go by illustrate this point: Generation
Y, the 9/11 Generation, the Facebook Generation, etc.[5]

From graduation commencement speeches, to youth conferences and missions conferences, millennials are sounded and bombarded with motivational messages about their new leadership and influential potential in the world. There seems to be a pricking up of ears to the need to understand who exactly this new brand of "world changers" are. According to Singer, Messera, and Orino:

> In 2011, a "silver tsunami" [hit] the United States: the oldest Baby Boomers will reach the United States legal retirement age of 65. As the Boomers leave the scene, a new generation will begin to take over.[6]

Already, the comparisons between the labels of baby boomers, Generation X, and Generation Y lends itself to the operational realms of stereotype threat, which is part of the point I seek to make in this section. Stereotype threat is intergenerational and itself impacts us all over the map. Since millennials are projected to assume leadership of world affairs, including missiological undertakings, what is being done to effectively train and equip them for the transitional stages to the challenging burden of shaping the world? Who is providing the safe space for this new emerging leadership to process their identity questions as exemplified by my friend Peter through his questions which I discuss in the following paragraphs? To this end, recently the corporate world has begun to realize that millennials bring new issues, new challenges, and new opportunities to the marketplace. Singer, Messera, and Orino's report show that

> indeed, a multi-billion dollar industry of firms has already sprung up around how best to teach, lead and integrate this new generation into the workplace. Those corporations that succeed at both utilizing the talents of the generation as well as marketing towards them, like Google has done so far, will thrive. Those that fail will be like the RCAs or Kodaks of past generations."[7]

But in my view the global missiological community is at risk of being the Kodaks of past generations. Effective practitioners in the helping vocations do not simply emerge; they are trained during certain experiences in life. Institutions, which have been entrusted with the preparation of millennials

5. Singer, Messera, and Orino, "D.C.'s New Guard."
6. Ibid.
7. Ibid.

for the vocation of helping, have given very little thought if any at all to this dynamic, up-and-coming generation. As an educator, consultant, and global practitioner who is aware of the complexities that surround the vocation of helping, I tend to develop my own suspicion as to whether millennials are professionally or not professionally prepared in a relevant, holistic manner for global complexities. But that's a discussion for another time.

Millennials or echo boomers, 2050

As clearly demonstrated in the previous chapters, stereotype threat affects people at any given intergenerational lineage, i.e., baby boomers, Xers, and millennials. As I focus on millennials, let me take you back to a couple of years ago, when I was invited to consult with a group of young, bright, and enthusiastic college students on the East Coast. I met with them at Battery Park in New York City. I was there to orient them in preparation for a summer study trip to Uganda. We bought our lunch from a Subway nearby and enjoyed the bloom of spring as we joked about and navigated all sorts of questions about international travel, cross-cultural communications, and intercultural imaginaries of life between American culture and life in Uganda. This was also an interesting time since the US media sphere and international news cycle was ablaze with the Joseph Kony 2012 saga. Here is what I have learned from many such interactions.

Millennial identity threat #1

Remember my friend Peter? I once asked him whether he was interested in traveling outside the United State on a short mission trip. Peter seemed willing, but he was strongly indifferent and hesitant to express any excitement about the possibility. Since I noticed his uneasiness with the answer he gave me, I asked him to tell me more. Peter mentioned the following: "I am a white, middle class, Christian, college-educated, American male, and I am the face of historic colonial oppression. When oppressed minorities are forced to abandon their identities and conform to the norm of the powerful majority, I am that norm. However, I want to do something to help the oppressed." What would your advice be for Peter? Get over it? Get over yourself and just do it? Before you are too quick to give Peter advice, assume a position of empathy. Have you ever felt like Peter, and do such questions restrict you from helping those in need? What does being preoccupied with such likelihoods mean for you? What does understanding the impact of such limiting thought processes mean for the way you approach opportunities to help your neighbors? Perhaps you did not know the consequences of such a degree of self-consciousness. I was intrigued by Peter's inquires and, in fact, he reminded me of similarly numerous curiosities I have fielded from groups and audiences filled with millennials, or "echo boomers," who have been told they should go and "change the world," "impact the world," and "save the world" through social justice.

One of the students I met, and who identifies as a millennial, lamented to me about his fears of being ineffective because as a young American he wants to save orphans but feels incapacitated by his worldview and Western background. He felt pressure to become involved in saving orphans in Africa and around the world because most of his friends had been on a trip to Mexico, Malawi, and Guatemala. He felt held back by something and he just did not know why the threat targeted him because of who he was. It seems to me that many people who feel the need to change the world, also tend to suffer from certain fears, anxiety, and pain. They are limited by an astounding persistence of uncertainty in their lives. They act like the hunted that do not know what to do, who they are, where they will live, and how to live up to their potential. The idea of "changing the world" sounds great, especially when you think of the accomplishments of acclaimed figures like Nelson Mandela, Steve Jobs, Mother Teresa, and Oprah. Yet, the processes of change continue to present uncertain realities because the dynamics of change are rapidly changing in and of themselves.

My response to Peter and anyone who finds themselves with similar inquires is an approach of empathy. Additionally, in respect to personal responsibility and personal leadership, I believe that you should resist the urge to seek the glory of impact first, and instead seek sisterhood and brotherhood. Before you seek to make an impact, can you try and be a friend, a sister, and a brother before you seek to be a hero? Try to extend a hand of friendship and thus engage in the journey of sisterhood or brotherhood. Realize that a "friend loves at all times but a brother or sister is born for adversity."[8] A person who is surrounded by vague and short-term oriented people will be abandoned, but "a real friend sticks closer than a brother."[9]

Now, regarding the unfortunate facts surrounding racial tension and colonialism's oppressive effects, it's important to acknowledge history and

8. Prov 17:17.
9. Prov 18:24.

learn from the past, but do not be bound by it. Distinctiveness is an integral facet of identity, but the fact of human similarity is to be cherished even more so. Don't dwell on yours or someone else's external differences, and therefore accentuate unnecessary effects of racialization. When it comes to helping in intercultural contexts, you need to equip yourself with social, emotional, and cultural intelligence in order to overcome the blind spots that emerge from a highly racialized social context. It is important for you to know your personal makeup as a person interested in helping in the area of global missions. Preparing may not provide all the answers you need, but during the process of preparation, one can acquire clues that will shape his or her responses. In certain intercultural situations, what a person does not know will lead to unfavorable results. As an intercultural specialist who is also credentialed with the Cultural Intelligence Center's training trainers certification and provides consultations for numerous groups, I encourage you to explore ways to raise your intercultural capabilities.

A sure area to look into is the field of cultural intelligence. It is a growing discipline that offers training opportunities to help people who are working cross-culturally to adapt relevantly to the host culture. David Livermore, who is the current president of the Cultural Intelligence Center, has written books about the need to be culturally intelligent. His books, which are relevant for this subject include, *The Cultural Intelligence Difference: Master the One Skill You Can't Do Without in Today's Global Economy*, *Serving With Eyes Wide Open: Doing Short-Term Missions With Cultural Intelligence*, and *Cultural Intelligence: Improving Your CQ to Engage Our Multicultural World*. In Livermore's literature, "Cultural intelligence is the capability to function effectively across national, ethnic, and organizational cultures."[10] In *Cultural Intelligence Difference*, Livermore writes about what he calls "research brief,"[11] which also introduces the reader to a "CQ self-assessment."[12] The capstone of cultural intelligence are the "strategies to improve your CQ;"[13] namely, "CQ drive, CQ knowledge, CQ strategy, and CQ action."[14]

---

10. Livermore, *Cultural Intelligence Difference*, Kindle loc., 157.

11. Ibid.

12. Ibid.

13. Ibid.

14. Ibid., 4–5.

Millennial identity threat #2

"I'm afraid I'll be mocked as a voluntourist."

Along with having cultural intelligence, which can serve to equip you with some tools in your desire to help, taking on the social identity of a volunteer also requires mindfulness. Peter also brought to my attention his hesitation with assuming the role of a volunteer in an international context. He was concerned that his "good intentions" might be caricatured as "volunteerism." What good does it do for him to travel to an underserved community? Isn't it better to send the money over to that particular community and let them do what is best with it? Indeed, Peter has every reason to be cautious about the nature of volunteer work and how it's done in many parts of the world, both at a local and global level.

A lot of mistakes have been made under the banner of volunteer work and thus there is the smoke of pain and embarrassment in volunteering stories that can be traced to legitimate fires. People who are interested in becoming volunteers need to be sure to do their homework by taking the time to study and become familiar with the areas in which they want to volunteer. I think that what people need to reconsider is the virtue of being generous with one's time in volunteering to the extent of giving their lives through relating to people as a priority. We live in a globalizing world that allows for being known and knowing people. This is critical for cultivating faithful friendships and acquiring a global eternal perspective. When you are relational and interdependent, you know who is credibly doing holistic work with measured impact and that's where your time and financial resources should go. When a man or woman who has experienced the love of God decides to be present with other people, there is nothing as generous as that and that is central to the activities of a volunteer. Volunteers are not perfect and it is necessary to admit that there will be shortcomings along the way. However, it is crucial to acknowledge that missional volunteers also have a sense for the need of connection to one another through principles like Ubuntu (Ubuntu is a word used in South Africa to remind us of our common humanity), hospitality, and the mutuality (Hebrew 13:1–3). Giving your time is primary and along with that flows the giving of resources. As you desire to volunteer, you should seek to join and partner with compassionate and competent leaders who research, test ideas, monitor, and constantly evaluate in order to achieve measured impact of behavioral change in their service to communities. Such an approach and vigilance will improve your volunteer experience and eliminate any possibilities of good intentions gone bad.

Chapter 9

Hope Abounds

IN THIS IS CHAPTER, I will labor to present various ways to redress the problem of stereotype threat unveiled in chapter one. From the apex of this section, it is essential to state the truth that hope in Jesus Christ, the gospel message, and His way reign supreme over any problem encountered in interethnic and intercultural partnerships. Scripture announces the good news and the magnanimous event of the cross it took Jesus to deliver God's love to the world. "For God so loved the world that he gave his one and only Son, that whoever believes in him shall not perish but have eternal life. For God did not send his Son into the world to condemn the world, but to save the world through him."[1]

Jesus' love, indeed, is the remedial reason for the expulsion of fears associated with any kind of threat that pervades the air and space of interethnic missional partnerships between Ugandans and Americans desiring partnership. In many instances, the scriptures instruct the reader to be fearless about mission strategies that fail to promote human flourishing and harmony. To this effect, the Bible asserts, "There is no fear in love. But perfect love drives out fear. . . . The one who fears is not made perfect in love."[2] Furthermore, fear in a cross-cultural context can be driven out through practical ways that derive their spiritual formal import from ascriptural commitment. The book of Timothy articulates, "God did not give us *a* spirit *of* fearfulness, but *of* power and love and *a* sound mind."[3] These divine instructions have been given to followers of Christ who make the church of Jesus Christ in both the local and global context. The current (Gal 3:23; Col

1. John 3:16–17.
2. 1 John 4:18.
3. 2 Tim 1:7.

3:11) and eschatological global church (Rev 7:9) is made up of ethnically, racially, culturally diverse ambassadors and disciples of Christ and this has implications for cross-cultural missions. However, as explained in the earlier parts of the study, people's encounters with different cultures in global missions tends to yield all sorts of outcomes.

What is culture and what makes up cultures? According to Heskett, culture is "the way we do things around here," is backed up by efforts to measure behavior and take some kind of corrective action when the behaviors are unacceptable to other members of a society or organization. These assumptions, values, beliefs, behaviors, artifacts, measurements, and actions determine how things get done in groups or organizations.[4] Followers of Jesus Christ, along with the rest of humanity, belong to communities around the world organized with sociocultural, political, economic, and spiritual dynamics that are impacted by stereotype threats. People in both their local and global societies depend on partnerships as mechanisms to accomplish similar tasks and goals.

The term "partnership" could mean many things and so it behooves me to state a definition of partnerships. "By definition, partnerships bring together different groups and individuals, and it is inevitable that there will be some tension, especially in situations in which there are historic conflicts based on fundamentally different cultural models."[5]

Any missionary group's ability to navigate and cross cultural borders for the purposes of forging interdependent partnerships is contingent on many aspects. For reiterative reasons, this world that God cares about is also impacted by the event of the fall of humanity. The book of Romans notes,

> For we have already made the charge that . . . all [are] under the
> power of sin. As it is written: "There is no one righteous, not even
> one; . . . there is no one who seeks God. All have turned away . . .
> for all have sinned and fall short of the glory of God."[6]

This leads to the difficulties in humanity's ability and capacity to relate, collaborate, and partner with one another along interethnic lines and cross-culturally. In this book, the challenge as stated in earlier chapters is the principle of stereotype threat, and cross-cultural missionaries involved in interethnic work cannot just wish and pray it out of the air. In fact, not

4. Heskett, *Culture Cycle*, 17.

5. Hora and Millar, *Guide to Building Education*, 79.

6. Rom 3:9–12.

even phrases like the following can do that:"'try twice as hard and ignore what other people think. . . . [Have] patience and endurance. . . . 'Just have faith' . . . and so on."[7]

The church of the twenty-first century as a global body commissioned to participate in God's mission, by way of sharing and enacting God's love, and the redemptive story of Jesus Christ in contextual ways, needs a paradigm shift. This book argues that stereotype threat in global church interethnic and interracial relationships between Ugandan Christians and Americans, where negative stereotyping can exist, can be prevented and alleviated through following the roads to faithful friendship and interdependent partnerships.

The impact of stereotype threat in missions has already been articulated and now the following ideas are practical roads of learning experiences that can bolster the process of building international cross-cultural partnerships. According to Dweck's ground-breaking study called *Mindset: The New Psychology of Success*, there is a difference between learning goals and performance goals. Learning goals are practical roads of growth to travel, while performance-driven goals are efforts from a fixed mind-set. After all, if you have it, you have it, and if you don't, you don't. However, the practical roads of learning experiences will position individuals toward growth mind-sets that lead to *aha!* experiences where one's cross-cultural qualities can be cultivated.[8]

Road 1: Reframing

Language is a direct channel through which stereotype threats are emitted and transmitted. The use of stereotypes, especially negative ones in cross-cultural spaces can increase people's vulnerability to identity threat. Therefore, it is crucial for missionaries on both the Ugandan and American sides to identify stereotype language and remove the cue that serves to trigger stereotype threat. The elimination of any communication infused with threats is paramount in missions and ministry-related tasks during the formation of interdependent partnerships across cultures. Scripture implores Christ's followers, especially those in a teaching position, to take precautions. James instructs,

7. Steele, *Whistling Vivaldi*, 154.

8. Dweck, *Mindset*, 10, 24.

Not many of you should become teachers, my fellow believers, because you know that we who teach will be judged more strictly. We all stumble in many ways. Anyone who is never at fault in what they say is perfect, able to keep their whole body in check. When we put bits into the mouths of horses to make them obey us, we can turn the whole animal. Or take ships, as an example. Although they are so large and are driven by strong winds, they are steered by a very small rudder wherever the pilot wants to go. Likewise, the tongue is a small part of the body, but it makes great boasts. Consider what a great forest is set on fire by a small spark. The tongue also is a fire, a world of evil among the parts of the body. Can both fresh water and salt water flow from the same spring? My brothers and sisters, can a fig tree bear olives, or a grapevine bear figs? Neither can a salt spring produce fresh water.[9]

Whether during the process of teaching theology or common interaction, stereotype happens in cross-cultural situations where social identities are singled out. Phrases like, "We are going to teach African pastors," "my orphan sponsor child," and so on need to be rethought and reframed because they heighten otherness. Woodley also raises other examples when he writes,

> The ethos of conquest as expressed in missional hegemony has become normalized in our times through the language of conquest. We go on "evangelistic crusades." We are taught to "win" others for Christ. We "make" a disciple. The Western worldview understands the binary choices in very clear and strategic terms. They (the cultural other) are lost and we are saved.[10]

When language is used in cross-cultural missions and the related tasks, it reflects values, attitudes, and beliefs of people. For example, one of the participants in this book's stereotype survey who is of American descent noted, "Africans have spirit, and we [Americans] have truth."[11] Admittedly, such generalizations are not an accurate representation of Americans, which underscores the need for consciousness-raising in missions. The discipline of discourse offers some hope in the direction of repentance and therefore reframing of language in cross-cultural missions. Potter and Wetherell note that if a certain negative attitude is expressed on one occasion, it should not necessarily determine one's inability to make the

9. Jas 3:1–12.

10. Woodley, "Mission and the Cultural Other," 7.

11. Paul Smith, interview by author, September 11, 2014, Portland, Oregon.

respectful changes.[12] Reframing and formulating language of solidarity and mutuality on both the Ugandan and American side can pave the way for reimagining fresh concepts that can aid faithful and friendly partnerships.

Road 2: De-emphasizing threatened social identities

Most Ugandan and American missionaries value their nationality and ethnic and cultural identities. These social identities can be conversational cultural intermediaries, but if not stewarded in a biblically reconciliatory, cross-cultural, and socially responsible way, they can lead to conflict. Global missions are characterized by constant interfacing of people from all walks of life and with diverse ethnic backgrounds.

Preventing and reducing stereotype threat requires the awareness of how and which identities are standardized to threat and the practice of the elimination of the threat. It is worth questioning what values might be added or subtracted when an American missionary is known by the term "muzungu," as it is defined in chapter one. Such a learning approach is not an endorsement of a performance-driven "strategic color blindness" tactic in cross-cultural missions.

According to research, color blindness is rooted in the belief that ethnic group membership and race-based differences should not be taken into account when decisions are made, impressions are formed, and behaviors are enacted.[13] Cross-cultural missionaries, who practice the art of knowing and being known in flexible ways as they relate and service people in intercultural contexts, can find encouragement in scripture. According to Paul, a posture of learning has a real advantage since one freely and happily becomes a servant of any to give testimony to Christ's love and the gospel. Paul further illustrates that when he is relationally present with people of Jewish culture and those of Gentile ethnicities, he seems as one with them while also bearing witness to the gospel.[14]

---

12. Potter and Wetherell, *Discourse and Social Psychology*, 45.

13. Apfelbaum, Norton, and Sommers, "Racial Color Blindness, 205.

14. 1 Cor 9:19–21.

Road 3: Introduce Christocentric training about self-perception beyond simplistic views of identity in missions

Among Christian circles and therefore missions, there is a generally shared self-identity in the term "Christian." This can be translated into one's identity being in Christ. However, areas of race, culture, and ethnicity are usually the tricky areas of identity to navigate in intercultural missions. To illustrate further, Richard Twiss, who is a Native American, narrates an experience that is appropriate in this regard. He writes,

> I remember that a few months after I had begun living at the training center in the beautiful Matanuska Valley north of Anchorage, I began to wonder how my Lakota heritage could be part of my new Christian experience. . . . So one afternoon I asked one of the pastoral leaders how I was supposed to relate to my Native culture as a Christian. I distinctly remember him opening the Bible he was carrying and reading from Galatians 3:28 (NIV), where Paul wrote, "There is nether Jew nor Greek, slave nor free, male nor female, for you are all one in Christ Jesus." After reading the passage, this pastoral leader commented on how cultures should all blend together for us as Christians He then concluded, "So, Richard, don't worry about being Indian; *just be like us.*[15]

Twiss's example demonstrates the complexities that surround identity in cross-cultural Christianity. In his story above, the pastor, was not able to satisfactorily answer the question at hand. Missionaries, who uphold and accept the various accidental differences inherent in people groups, are positioned to positively participate in the development of intercultural partnerships. Research notes that individuals who actively participated both intellectually and emotionally in the process of identifying uniting characteristics shared by in-group and out-group members, in particular threatened domains, appeared to be less vulnerable to developing stereotype threat in conditions that normally produce it.[16]

In Uganda, the utilization of a cardinal and the culturally inbred social imagination of *ubuntu,* which means *shared humanness,* is highly advantageous in forming positive partnerships and ultimately faithful friendships. Cross-cultural groups can adapt a satisfying interethnic framework as a

---

15. Twiss, *One Church, Many Tribes,* 34.
16. Rosenthal, Crisp, and Suen, "Improving Performance Expectancies," 588.

beginning place aimed at attenuating stereotype threat. According to Orbe and Harris, the following are practical themes groups can discuss:

Worldview theme: It involves sharing common experience and interests seen as crucial to communication satisfaction. When it come to worldviews, the parties involved in building partnerships and faithful friendships should resist the temptation to assume in a prejudging manner that one's outlook is better than the other. It is absolutely significant to seek to listen and try to understand before you are understood.

Acceptance theme: This is where interethnic interactions are regarded as satisfying because of the perception that one's ideas and culture were accepted, confirmed, and respected.

Negative stereotypes: This is a main source of dissatisfying interethnic relationship and communication. Being categorized solely through the limits of ethnicity only (as opposed to being seen as a whole person and human being loved and created by God) creates barriers between persons.

Relational solidarity: Relates to the positive values attributed to developing close intercultural and faithful friendships.

Expressiveness: Interethnic communication was characterized as satisfying when a comfortable climate was developed by both parties. In other words, individuals could express themselves openly, honestly, and fully without a fear of rejection, judgment, or retaliation.[17]

Road 4: Elevate positive contextual role models from diverse groups

Most missions groups from the United States tend not to be ethically diverse. Yet the desire for diversity for diversity's sake is not productive. However, partnerships between Ugandans and Americans by nature lead to and involve an experience of God's love and presence in ethnically diverse communities. Diversity already exists naturally as a fact, not a sought-after goal. A positive experience of Christocentric diverse settings can nurture a joyful ethos of unity. Scripture reassures, "How wonderful it is, how pleasant,

---

17. Orbe and Harris, *Interracial Communication*, 299.

when brothers [and sisters] live in harmony!"[18] Christ's love breaks down barriers and builds up communities of people. When people on missions can be thankful for their unique quality and cherish difference in the self in relation to the other, positive outcomes are likely.

Studies also show that by reducing category-differentiation, the boundaries between groups become blurred and the representation of the two groups overlap. Strategies that reduce category differentiation remove one of the cognitive prerequisites for intergroup bias. Reducing the distinction between "us" and "them" means that "they" cannot be evaluated less positively than "us." Thus far, research in intergroup relations suggests that reducing category differentiation can decrease explicit bias.[19]

Stereotype threat is an affront to the already prevailing love of God. Positive and diverse role models can avert threats. The unique emphasis here on the elevation of positive and diverse role models in cross-cultural missions partnership contexts are significant for the following reasons. According to researchers, the effectiveness of a successful in-group role model might be not in attributes of the person but rather in attributions made by the perceiver, using well-known principles of causal attribution. According to attribution theories, "deservingness" is defined as having achieved success through causes that are relatively internal rather than external, and stable rather than unstable.[20]

Cross-cultural mission organizations and churches need inclusive structures. Otherwise, stereotype threat will conformably enjoy the atmospheric warmth that the absence of positive, diverse, and contextual role models provide. The numbers of missionaries who are sent and travel to Uganda on both short- and long-term missions overwhelmingly favor the demographic presentation of the majority culture of America. How are partnerships supposed to equitably form without prior experience with members of diverse groups in one's local setting or national context? Most importantly, since cross-cultural partnerships are formed for the benefit of diverse groups, doesn't it follow then that the partnerships reflect the diverse opinions, cultures, and various input?

18. Psalm 133:1.

19. Rosenthal, Crisp, and Suen, "Improving Performance Expectancies."

20. Taylor et al., "Hillary Clinton effect," 449.

Road 5: Provide affirmation and care for attributions

The emotional stakes are high for people under stereotype threat. Some of the emotional outcomes range from dejection, sadness, anxiety, shame, confusion, and guilt. A collaborative approach to pastoral guidance can play a pivotal role in undermining the effect of threats. Sometimes, the origins and reasons of conflict from threatening situations require explanation. Schmidt argues that a collaborative style of communication recognizes the productive potential of conflict and encourages people to engage in dialogue thoughtfully. This is active affirmation of the importance of relationships and the partner approach.[21]

Through counseling, explanation, comfort, and prayer, Elmer suggests the use of a strategy called "carefronting."[22] He further comments that carefronting means directly approaching the other person in a caring way so that achieving a win-win solution is most likely. With this approach, neither party loses anything important and the relationship does not suffer. However, several conditions must be met to achieve a mutual win-win situation through carefronting.[23] Elmer additionally offers practical ways to conduct the process of caring for people who are experiencing an identity threat in the cross-cultural context. It is arguably the case that carefronting also seeks to flesh out the principles from the Scriptures. According to Matthew,

> If a brother sins against you, go to him privately and confront him with his fault. If he listens and confesses it, you have won back a brother. But if not, then take one or two others with you and go back to him again, proving everything you say by these witnesses. If he still refuses to listen, then take your case to the church.[24]

Elmer's steps are:

- The two parties can come together, meet face-to-face and talk with open honesty.
- They each make a commitment to preserve the relationship and dispassionately explain the values/goals that each wishes to protect or achieve.

21. Schmidt, *Communicating Globally*, 110–11.
22. Elmer, *Cross-Cultural Conflict*, 42.
23. Ibid., 43.
24. Matt 18:15–17.

- They can creatively find a solution in which they both equally understand one another, while neither one gives up anything of value, and thus preserves the relationship.

- They can do this with reason, keeping emotions under control.

- They are both able to separate the person from the issue and speak objectively to that end.

- Neither will be satisfied with a solution until the other is also completely at peace with it.[25]

Other pointers and questions to prayerfully reflect on and that are helpful to ponder over and can serve to arouse one's empathy and compassion particularly in non-western contexts like Uganda are:

- Be a prayerful person; cherish the story of Jesus Christ by being a witness of the gospel.

- Practice the art of peripheral discernment and maturity (1 Cor 13

- Be open and willing to be known, to know, and to listen to the other person's views.

- Practice generosity by building up people and families with no strings attached.

- Practice self-leadership both in private and public life.

- How conscious are you about the cultural motifs, respectfulness, honor, and composure?

- Are you willing to acquire basic indigenous languages and a cultural idiom since they are clear doors into cultures skills?

- Practice forgiveness and mercy. Avoid unhealthy habits of withdrawal and bitterness in your heart.

Along with all the practical roads that have been suggested in the preceding part of this chapter, it is helpful to consider the theological understanding of missions that need to be reframed and revised. The notion that "missionaries bring God" to other cultures needs to be questioned since the assumptions upon which notions are based tend to be grounded in ethnocentrism, rather than a global perspective with a unshakable belief in God's omnipresence.

25. Elmer, *Cross-Cultural Conflict*, 43.

Randy Woodley's guidelines for missions

In favor of a paradigm shift in missions, Woodley proposes missiological guidelines that are worthy of reflection and implementation in missions education and practices. Woodley's ten guidelines are:

- There is no place we can go where Jesus is not already present and active. Jesus is eventually recognized by many of the writers of the New Testament as Creator. The efficacy of Christ in creation as Creator (John 1:1–4, 1:10–14; Col 1:15–20; 1 Cor 8:6; Heb 1:1), the fact that God has always had a covenantal relationship with all peoples (Amos 9:7), the fact that Jesus is the truth, meaning all truth points to him and he fulfills all truth: these facts point to the inescapable reality that Jesus is present everywhere.

- Since Jesus is present and active everywhere, the first responsibility of mission among any culture is not to teach, speak, or exert privilege but to discover what Jesus is doing in that culture (John 5:19).

- Realize God expects two conversions out of every missional encounter: (1) our conversion to the truths in their culture, and (2) their conversion to the truth we bring to the encounter (Luke 7:36–50, 10:25–37).

- Our humility as servants of Jesus should naturally lead us to convert first to the truths in their culture everywhere we see Jesus at work (Acts 10:23–48).

- Through the work of culture guides (people of that culture), earnest study, prayer, and experiential failures, it is our responsibility to first adapt to and then embrace their culture, and as much as possible, their worldview (Acts 17).

- Realize that conversion is both instantaneous and a process, and think through those implications as we begin to consider our timelines. Then, throw out our timelines (Rom 13:11).

- During this time, also read, study, and discuss with others ways that you can continue to deconstruct your own worldview and culture. This is a long, painful, and yet freeing process (Eph 4:23; Rom 12:2).

- Our own process of conversion may take years, so be patient with yourself and with God (Gal 2:12).

- When, and if, they invite us to share the gospel they have noticed us living out, then the process formally known as cultural contextualization should occur (1 Cor 9:20).

- Their process of conversion may take years, so be patient (Eph 4:2).[26]

Conclusion

Claude Steele, along with other stereotype threat researchers, have and continue to provide formidable information about the nature of stereotype threat. This book labors to propose the need to consider the role that stereotype threat plays in interethnic, cross-cultural, and intercultural settings of the global church's mission events. Awareness about stereotype threat and the necessary practical ways to counter it in both local and global church communities is beneficial for living harmoniously and for the holistic practice of mission. The practice of global missions will improve with the consistent reevaluation of old structures, which pave the way to reduction of conflict and to the realization of harmony. Although stereotype threat is a destabilizing force to relationships in cross-cultural contexts, willing minds and open hearts can be set to God's invitation to love the Lord your God with all your heart and with all your soul, strength, mind, and love your neighbor.[27] When the call to love God and people is answered, adherence to God and positive decisions and movements toward the Creator and humanity follow. With the Creator's empowerment and the utilization of research, followers of Christ can prevent and alleviate stereotype threat in global church interethnic and interracial relationships between Ugandan Christians and Americans and elsewhere, and thus, the constructive experience of partnership begins.

26. Woodley, "Mission and the Cultural Other," 465.

27. Luke 10:27.

Bibliography

Acemoglu, Daron, and James A. Robinson. *Why Nations Fail: The Origins of Power, Prosperity and Poverty*. New York: Crown, 2012.

Achebe, Chinua. *The Education of a British-Protected Child*. New York: Knopf, 2009.

Adams, John. *A Biography in His Own Words*. Edited by James Bishop Peabody. New York: Newsweek, 1973.

Amstutz, Mark R. *Evangelicals and American Foreign Policy*. Oxford: Oxford University Press, 2014.

Apfelbaum, Evan P., Michael I. Norton, and Samuel R. Sommers. "Racial Color Blindness: Emergence, Practice, and Implications." *Current Directions in Psychological Science* 21 (2012) 205–9.

Aronson, Joshua, Carrie B. Fried, and Catherine Good. "Reducing the Effects of Stereotype Threat on African American College Students by Shaping Theories of Intelligence." *Journal of Experimental Social Psychology* 38 (2002) 113–25.

Bachmann-Medick, Doris, ed. *The Trans/National Study of Culture: A Translational Perspective*. Concepts for the Study of Culture 4. Boston: De Gruyter, 2014.

Bamforth, Douglas B. "Indigenous People, Indigenous Violence: Precontact Warfare on the North American Great Plains." *Man* 29 (1994) 95–115.

Barát, Erzsébet, Patrick Studer, and Jiří Nekvapil, eds. *Ideological Conceptualizations of Language: Discourses of Linguistic Diversity*. Prague Papers on Language, Society and Interaction 3. New York: Peter Lang, 2013.

Barkham, Patrick. "Taking the Risk Out of Being a Good Samaritan." *Guardian*, November 19, 2009. https://www.theguardian.com/society/2009/nov/19/good-samaritan-fear-of-helping.

Becker, Arthur H. *Guilt: Curse or Blessing?* Minneapolis: Augsburg, 1977.

Bediako, Kwame. *Christianity in Africa: The Renewal of a Non-Western Religion*. Edinburgh: Edinburgh University Press, 1995.

———. *Theology and Identity: The Impact of Culture Upon Christian Thought in the Second Century and in Modern Africa*. Oxford: Regnum, 1999.

Beidelman, T. O. *Colonial Evangelism: A Socio-Historical Study of an East African Mission at the Grassroots*. Bloomington: Indiana University Press, 1982.

Bizimana, Nsekuye. *White Paradise, Hell for Africa?* Berlin: Edition Humana, 1989.

Bonk, Jonathan. *Missions and Money: Affluence as a Missionary Problem—Revisited*. American Society of Missiology 15. Maryknoll, NY: Orbis, 2006.

Borthwick, Paul. *Western Christians in Global Mission: What's the Role of the North American Church?* Downers Grove, IL: InterVarsity, 2012.

Bosch, David J. *Transforming Mission: Paradigm Shifts in Theology of Missions.* Maryknoll, NY: Orbis, 1991.

Boyer, Paul, et al. *The Enduring Vision: A History of the American People.* Boston: Wadsworth, 2013.

Burrows, William R., Mark R. Gornik, and Janice A. McLean, eds. *Understanding World Christianity: The Vision and Work of Andrew F. Walls.* Maryknoll, NY: Orbis, 2011.

Carter, Craig A. *Rethinking Christ and Culture: A Post-Christendom Perspective.* Grand Rapids: Brazos, 2006.

Carter, Mia, and Barbara Harlow, eds. *Archives of Empire.* Vol. 2, *The Scramble for Africa.* Durham: Duke University Press, 2003.

Chang, Larry, ed. *Wisdom for the Soul: Five Millennia of Prescriptions for Spiritual Healing.* Washington, DC: Gnosophia, 2006.

Collier, Paul. *The Bottom Billion: Why the Poorest Countries Are Failing and What Can Be Done About It.* New York: Oxford University Press, 2007.

Collins, Gary R. *Christian Counseling: A Comprehensive Guide.* London: Word Publishing, 1988.

Concannon, Kevin, Francisco A. Lomelí, and Marc Priewe, eds. *Imagined Transnationalism: U. S. Latino/a Literature, Culture, and Identity.* New York: Palgrave Macmillan, 2009.

Crabtree, Steve. "Religiosity Highest in World's Poorest Nations." *Gallup,* August 31, 2010. http://www.gallup.com/poll/142727/religiosity-highest-world-poorest-nations.aspx.

Cuffel, Alexandra, and Brian M. Britt, eds. *Religion, Gender, and Culture in the Pre-Modern World.* New York: Palgrave Macmillan, 2007.

Curtin, Philip DeArmond. *The Image of Africa: British Ideas and Action, 1780–1850.* Vol. 1. Madison: University of Wisconsin Press, 1973.

Dalakar, Joseph. "Poverty in the United States in 2015: In Brief." Congressional Research Service, October 4, 2016. https://fas.org/sgp/crs/misc/R44644.pdf.

Damron, Neil. "Poverty Fact Sheet: Brain Drain: A Child's Brain on Poverty." Institute for Research on Poverty, University of Wisconsin–Madison, n.d. https://morgridge.wisc.edu/documents/Brain_Drain_A_Childs_Brain_on_Poverty.pdf

Darity, William, Jr., and Dania Frank. "The Economics of Reparations." *American Economic Review* 93 (May 2003) 326–29.

Davies, Paul G., Steven J. Spencer, and Claude M. Steele. "Clearing the Air: Identity Safety Moderates the Effects of Stereotype Threat on Women's Leadership Aspirations." *Journal Of Personality and Social Psychology* 88 (2005) 276–87.

Davis-Maye, Denise, Annice D. Yarber, and Tonya E. Perry, eds. *What the Village Gave Me: Conceptualizations of Womanhood.* Lanham, MD: University Press of America, 2014.

Deaux, Kay, et al. "Becoming American: Stereotype Threat Effects in Afro-Caribbean Immigrant Groups." *Social Psychology Quarterly* 70 (2007) 384–404.

De Becker, Gavin. *The Gift of Fear: And Other Survival Signals That Protect Us from Violence.* Boston: Little, Brown, 1997.

Dowden, Richard. *Africa: Altered States, Ordinary Miracles.* New York: Public Affairs, 2009.

Dweck, Carol. *Mindset: The New Psychology of Success.* New York: Random House, 2006.

Eades, Gwilym Lucas. *Maps and Memes: Redrawing Culture, Place, and Identity in Indigenous Communities.* Montreal: McGill-Queen's University Press, 2015.

Elmer, Duane. *Cross-Cultural Conflict: Building Relationships for Effective Ministry.* Downers Grove, IL: InterVarsity, 1994.

Farmer, Paul. *AIDS and Accusation: Haiti and the Geography of Blame.* Berkeley: University of California Press, 2006.

Fikkert, Brian, and Steve Corbett. *When Helping Hurts: How to Alleviate Poverty Without Hurting the Poor—And Yourself.* Chicago: Moody, 2009.

Flippen, Alan. " Where Are the Hardest Places to Live in the U. S.?" *New York Times,* June 26, 2014. https://www.nytimes.com/2014/06/26/upshot/where-are-the-hardest-places-to-live-in-the-us.html?abt=0002&abg=1&_r=1.

Frantz, Cynthia M., et al. "A Threat in the Computer: The Race Implicit Association Test as a Stereotype Threat Experience." *Personality and Social Psychology Bulletin* 30 (2004) 1610–24.

Friedman, Edwin H. *A Failure of Nerve: Leadership in the Age of the Quick Fix.* New York: Church Publishing, 2007.

Gilley, Sheridan, and Brian Stanley, eds. *World Christianity, C. 1815–1914.* The Cambridge History of Christianity 8. Cambridge: Cambridge University Press, 2006.

Glassner, Barry. *The Culture of Fear: Why Americans Are Afraid of the Wrong Things.* New York: Basic Books, 2009.

Goffman, Erving. *Stigma: Notes on the Management of Spoiled Identity.* Englewood Cliffs, NJ: Prentice-Hall, 1963.

Gordon-Conwell Theological Seminary. "Christianity 2015: Religious Diversity and Personal Contact." *International Bulletin of Mission Research* 39 (2015) 28–29. http://www.gordonconwell.edu/ockenga/research/documents/2IBMR2015.pdf.

Grillo, John L., and Cameron Ruth Tonkiss, eds. "World Missionary Conference Records, Edinburgh, 1910." Burke Library Archives, Union Theological Seminary, New York, June 1910. http://www.columbia.edu/cu/lweb/img/assets/6398/MRL12_WMC_FA.pdf.

Gudykunst, William B., and Young Yun Kim. *Communicating with Strangers: An Approach to Intercultural Communication.* New York: Random House, 1984.

Hall, Erika. "Whites View the Term 'African-American' More Favorably than 'Black.'" *Washington Post,* November 18, 2014. https://www.washingtonpost.com/news/wonk/wp/2014/11/18/whites-view-the-term-african-american-more-favorably-than-black/?utm_term=.e6c32bf8352e.

Harlow, Barbara, and Mia Carter, eds. *Archives of Empire.* Vol. 2, *The Scramble for Africa.* Durham: Duke University Press, 2003.

Hastings, Adrian. *Church and Mission in Modern Africa.* London: Burns and Oates, 1967.
———. *The Church in Africa: 1450–1950.* New York: Oxford University Press, 1994.

Hegel, Georg Wilhelm Friedrich. *The Philosophy of History.* Translated by J. Sibree. New York: Dover, 1956.

Heskett, James. *The Culture Cycle: How to Shape the Unseen Force that Transforms Performance.* Upper Saddle River, NJ: FT Press, 2012.

Hiebert, Paul G. *Anthropological Insights for Missionaries.* Grand Rapids: Baker, 1985.
———. *Anthropological Reflections on Missiological Issues.* Grand Rapids: Baker, 1994.
———. *Cultural Anthropology.* Philadelphia: Lippincott, 1976.
———. *The Gospel in Human Contexts: Anthropological Explorations for Contemporary Missions.* Grand Rapids: Baker Academic, 2009.
———. *The Missiological Implications of Epistemological Shifts Affirming Truth in a Modern/Postmodern World.* Harrisburg, PA: Trinity Press, 1999.

———. *Transforming Worldviews: An Anthropological Understanding of How People Change*. Grand Rapids: Baker Academic, 2008.

Hiebert, Paul G., and Eloise Hiebert Meneses. *Incarnational Ministry: Planting Churches in Band, Tribal, Peasant, and Urban Societies*. Grand Rapids: Baker, 1995.

Hiebert, Paul G., and Frances F. Hiebert. *Case Studies in Missions*. Grand Rapids: Baker, 1987.

Hiebert, Paul G., and R. Daniel Shaw. *The Power and the Glory: A Missiological Approach to the Study of Religion*. Pasadena, CA: Hiebert and Shaw, 1993.

Hiebert, Paul G., R. Daniel Shaw, and Tite Tienou. *Understanding Folk Religion: A Christian Response to Popular Beliefs and Practices*. Grand Rapids: Baker, 1999.

Hora, Matthew, and Susan B. Millar. *A Guide to Building Education Partnerships: Navigating Diverse Cultural Contexts to Turn Challenge into Promise*. Sterling, VA: Stylus, 2011.

Hunt, June. *Guilt: Living Guilt Free*. Torrance, CA: Rose Publishing, 2013.

Inzlicht, Michael, and Toni Schmader, eds. *Stereotype Threat: Theory, Process, and Application*. New York: Oxford University Press, 2012.

James, Larry M. *The Wealth of the Poor: How Valuing Every Neighbor Restores Hope in Our Cities*. Abilene, TX: Abilene Christian University Press, 2013.

Jenkins, Philip. *The Next Christendom: The Coming of Global Christianity*. New York: Oxford University Press, 2011.

Johnson, Bernice Koehler. *The Shan: Refugees Without a Camp—An English Teacher in Thailand and Burma*. Paramus, NJ: Trinity Matrix, 2009.

Keim, Curtis A. *Mistaking Africa: Curiosities and Inventions of the American Mind*. Boulder, CO: Westview, 2009.

Kern, Stephen. *The Culture of Time and Space 1880–1918*. Cambridge: Harvard University Press, 1983.

Kim, Young Yun. *Becoming Intercultural: An Integrative Theory of Communication and Cross-Cultural Adaptation*. Thousand Oaks, CA: SAGE, 2001.

King, Martin Luther, Jr., "Letter from Birmingham Jail." Martin Luther King, Jr., Research and Education Institute, April 16, 1963. http://okra.stanford.edu/transcription/document_images/undecided/630416-019.pdf.

Kristof, Nicholas. "Following God Abroad." *New York Times*, May 21, 2002. http://www.nytimes.com/2002/05/21/opinion/following-god-abroad.html.

Kroeber, A. L. and Clyde Kluckhohn. *Culture: A Critical Review of Concepts and Definitions*. Cambridge: The Museum, 1952.

Kyeyune, Stephen. *The Legacy of a Hero: Life Lived from the Christian Prospective*. Bloomington, IN: AuthorHouse, 2013.

"The Lausanne Covenant." Lausanne Movement, August 1, 1974. https://www.lausanne.org/content/covenant/lausanne-covenant.

LeDoux, Joseph E. *Anxious: Using the Brain to Understand and Treat Fear and Anxiety*. New York: Viking, 2015.

———. "Emotion: Clues From the Brain." *Annual Review of Psychology* 46 (1995) 209–35.

Lewis, Donald M., ed. *Christianity Reborn: The Global Expansion of Evangelicalism in the Twentieth Century*. Grand Rapids: Eerdmans, 2004.

Lin, Ann, and David R. Harris. *The Colors of Poverty: Why Racial and Ethnic Disparities Persist*. New York: Russell Sage, 2008.

Lingenfelter, Sherwood G. *Agents of Transformation: A Guide for Effective Cross-Cultural Ministry*. Grand Rapids: Baker, 1996.

———. *Leading Cross-Culturally: Covenant Relationships for Effective Christian Leadership.* Grand Rapids: Baker Academic, 2008.

Lingenfelter, Sherwood G., and Marvin Keene Mayers. *Ministering Cross-Culturally: An Incarnational Model for Personal Relationships.* Grand Rapids: Baker, 1986.

Little, Brian R. *Me, Myself, and Us: The Science of Personality and the Art of Well-Being.* Toronto: HarperCollins, 2014.

Livermore, David A. *The Cultural Intelligence Difference: Master the One Skill You Can't Do Without in Today's Global Economy.* New York: American Management Association, 2011.

———. *Expand Your Borders: Discover Ten Cultural Clusters.* CQ Insight Series 1. East Lansing, MI: Cultural Intelligence Center, 2013.

———. *Leading with Cultural Intelligence: The New Secret to Success.* New York: American Management Association, 2010.

———. *Serving with Eyes Wide Open: Doing Short-Term Missions with Cultural Intelligence.* Grand Rapids: Baker, 2006.

Loury, Glenn C. *The Anatomy of Racial Inequality.* Cambridge: Harvard University Press, 2002.

Lybrand, Fred R. *About Life and Uganda: Insights from a Short-Term Pilgrim.* Victoria, Canada: Trafford, 2003.

MacLeod, Ray, and Philip F. Rehbock, eds. *Darwin's Laboratory: Evolutionary Theory and Natural History in the Pacific.* Honolulu: University of Hawaii'i Press, 1994.

Mamdani, Mahmood. *Beyond Rights Talk and Culture Talk: Comparative Essays on the Politics of Rights and Culture.* New York: St. Martin's, 2000.

———. *Define and Rule: Native As Political Identity.* Cambridge: Harvard University Press, 2012.

McCarthy, Michael. *Dark Continent: Africa as Seen by Americans.* Westport, CT: Greenwood, 1983.

Moyo, Dambisa. *Dead Aid: Why Aid is Not Working and How There is a Better Way for Africa.* New York: Farrar, Straus and Giroux, 2009.

Mutibwa, Phares Mukasa. *Uganda Since Independence: A Story of Unfulfilled Hopes.* Trenton, NJ: Africa World Press, 1992.

Nakata, Cheryl, ed. *Beyond Hofstede: Culture Frameworks for Global Marketing and Management.* London: Palgrave Macmillan, 2009.

National Geographic Visual Atlas of the World. Washington, DC: National Geographic Society, 2009.

Nelson, Jack E. *Christian Missionizing and Social Transformation: A History of Conflict and Change in Eastern Zaire.* New York: Praeger, 1992.

Obama, Barack. *Dreams From My Father: A Story of Race and Inheritance.* New York: Three Rivers Press, 2004.

Offutt, Stephen, et al. *Advocating for Justice: An Evangelical Vision for Transforming Systems and Structures.* Grand Rapids: Baker Academic, 2016.

Olopade, Dayo. *The Bright Continent: Breaking Rules and Making Change in Modern Africa.* Boston: Houghton Mifflin, 2014.

Orbe, Mark P., and Tina M. Harris. *Interracial Communication: Theory into Practice.* Belmont, CA: Wadsworth, 2001.

Ott, Craig, and Harold A. Netland, eds. *Globalizing Theology: Belief and Practice in an Era of World Christianity.* Grand Rapids: Baker Academic, 2006.

Pakenham, Thomas. *The Scramble for Africa: White Man's Conquest of the Dark Continent from 1876–1912*. New York: Random House, 1991.

Pinel, Elizabeth C. "Stigma Consciousness: The Psychological Legacy of Social Stereotypes." *Journal of Personality and Social Psychology* 76 (1999) 114–28.

Pittinsky, Todd L. *Us Plus Them: Tapping the Positive Power of Difference*. Boston: Harvard Business Review Press, 2012.

Potter, Jonathan, and Margaret Wetherell. *Discourse and Social Psychology: Beyond Attitudes and Behaviour*. London: SAGE, 1987.

"Poverty Status Report 2014: Structural Change and Poverty Reduction in Uganda." Economic Development Policy and Research Department: Ministry of Finance, Planning and Economic Development, November 2014. http://www.ug.undp.org/content/dam/uganda/docs/UNDPUg2014%20-%20POVERTY%20STATUS%20REPORT%202014.compressed.pdf.

Priest, Robert J., and Alvaro L. Nieves, eds. *This Side of Heaven: Race, Ethnicity, and Christian Faith*. Oxford: Oxford University Press, 2007.

Pronin, Emily, Claude M. Steele, and Lee Ross. "Identity Bifurcation in Response to Stereotype Threat: Women and Mathematics." *Journal of Experimental Social Psychology* 40 (2004) 152–68.

Rarick, Charles, et al. "An Investigation of Ugandan Cultural Values and Implications for Managerial Behavior." *Global Journal of Management and Business Research* 13 (2013) 1–10. https://globaljournals.org/GJMBR_Volume13/1-An-Investigation-of-Ugandan-Cultural.pdf.

"Remarks by President Obama at the Global Entrepreneurship Summit." White House, July 25, 2015. https://www.whitehouse.gov/the-press-office/2015/07/25/remarks-president-obama-global-entrepreneurship-summit.

Remland, Martin S., et al. *Intercultural Communication: A Peacebuilding Perspective*. Long Grove, IL: Waveland, 2015.

Ripken, Nik. "What's Wrong with Western Missionaries?" *DesiringGod*, September 12, 2016. http://www.desiringgod.org/articles/what-s-wrong-with-western-missionaries.

Robert, Dana Lee, ed. *Converting Colonialism: Visions and Realities in Mission History, 1706–1914*. Grand Rapids: Eerdmans, 2008.

Roosevelt, Theodore. *African Game Trails: An Account of the African Wanderings of an American Hunter-Naturalist*. Santa Barbara, CA: Narrative Press, 2001.

Rosenthal, Harriet E. S., Richard J. Crisp, and Mein-Woei Suen. "Improving Performance Expectancies in Stereotypic Domains: Task Relevance and the Reduction of Stereotype Threat." *European Journal of Social Psychology* 37 (2007) 586–97.

Rothenberg, Paula S., ed. *White Privilege: Essential Readings on the Other Side of Racism*. New York: Worth, 2002.

Russell, Bertrand. *Sceptical Essays*. London: Routledge, 2004.

Saad, Carmel S., et al. "Domain Identification Moderates the Effect of Positive Stereotypes on Chinese American Women's Math Performance." *Cultural Diversity and Ethnic Minority Psychology* 21 (2006) 162–67.

Said, Edward W. *Culture and Imperialism*. New York: Knopf, 1993.

———. *Power, Politics, and Culture: Interviews with Edward W. Said*. Edited by Gauri Viswanathan. New York: Pantheon, 2001.

Said, Edward W., and David Barsamian. *Culture and Resistance: Conversations with Edward W. Said*. Cambridge: South End Press, 2003.

Sanneh, Lamin O. *Abolitionists Abroad: American Blacks and the Making of Modern West Africa.* Cambridge: Harvard University Press, 1999.

———. *Disciples of All Nations: Pillars of World Christianity.* New York: Oxford University Press, 2008.

———. *Encountering the West: Christianity and the Global Cultural Process: The African Dimension.* Maryknoll, NY: Orbis, 1993.

———. *Translating the Message: The Missionary Impact on Culture.* Maryknoll, NY: Orbis, 1989.

———. *Whose Religion Is Christianity?: The Gospel Beyond the West.* Grand Rapids: Eerdmans, 2003.

Sanneh, Lamin O., and Joel A. Carpenter, eds. *The Changing Face of Christianity Africa, the West, and the World.* New York: Oxford University Press, 2005.

Schipper, Mineke. *Imagining Insiders: Africa and the Question of Belonging.* New York: Cassell, 1999.

Schmader, Toni, Brenda Major, and Richard W. Gramzow. "Coping With Ethnic Stereotypes in the Academic Domain: Perceived Injustice and Psychological Disengagement." *Journal of Social Issues* 57 (2001) 93–111.

Schmidt, Wallace V. *Communicating Globally: Intercultural Communication and International Business.* Los Angeles: SAGE, 2007.

Schneider, David J. *The Psychology of Stereotyping.* New York: Guilford, 2004.

Schulzinger, Robert D. *U. S. Diplomacy Since 1900.* New York: Oxford University Press, 2008.

Sen, Sudipta. *Distant Sovereignty: National Imperialism and the Origins of British India.* New York: Routledge, 2002.

Seuss, Dr. *The Lorax.* New York: Random House, 1971.

Sharifian, Farzad, et al., eds. *Culture, Body, and Language: Conceptualizations of Internal Body Organs Across Cultures and Languages.* Berlin: De Gruyter, 2008.

"Short-Term Mission Trips: Are They Worth the Investment?" Baylor University, May 2, 2011. http://www.baylor.edu/mediacommunications/news.php?action=story&story=93238.

Singer, Peter W., Heather L. Messera, and Brendan Orino. "D.C.'s New Guard: What Does the Next Generation of American Leaders Think?" *Brookings,* February 24, 2011. https://www.brookings.edu/research/d-c-s-new-guard-what-does-the-next-generation-of-american-leaders-think/.

Smith, Christian, et al. *American Evangelicalism: Embattled and Thriving.* Chicago: University of Chicago Press, 1998.

Southern Poverty Law Center. "The Trump Effect: The Impact of the Presidential Campaign on Our Nation's Schools," April 13, 2016. https://www.splcenter.org/20160413/trump-effect-impact-presidential-campaign-our-nations-schools.

Soyinka-Airewele, Peyi, and Rita Kiki Edozie, eds. *Reframing Contemporary Africa: Politics, Economics, and Culture in the Global Era.* Washington, DC: CQ Press, 2010.

Stambach, Amy. *Faith in Schools: Religion, Education, and American Evangelicals in East Africa.* Stanford: Stanford University Press, 2010.

Stearns, Richard. *The Hole in Our Gospel.* Nashville: Thomas Nelson, 2009.

Steele, Claude M. "Steele Discusses Stereotype Threat." *College Street Journal,* September 24, 2004. https://www.mtholyoke.edu/offices/comm/csj/092404/steele.shtml.

———. "Stereotyping and Its Threat Are Real." *American Psychologist* 53 (1998) 680–81.

———. "A Threat in the Air: How Stereotypes Shape Intellectual Identity and Performance." *American Psychologist* 52 (1997) 613–29.

———. *Whistling Vivaldi: How Stereotypes Affect Us, and What We Can Do*. New York: Norton, 2011.

Steele, Claude M., and Joshua Aronson. "Stereotype Threat and the Intellectual Test." *Journal of Personality and Social Psychology* 69 (1995) 797–811.

Steffan, Melissa. "The Surprising Countries Most Missionaries Are Sent From and Go To." *Christianity Today*, July 25, 2013.

"Stereotype Threat Affects Women in High-Level Math Courses, Aronson Study Finds." New York University, Department of Applied Psychology, January 29, 2008. http://steinhardt.nyu.edu/news/2008/1/29/Stereotype_Threat_Affects_Women_in_Highlevel_Math_Courses_Aronson_Study_Finds.

Steyn, Hansie. *The King Saul Spirit*. Maitland, FL: Xulon Press, 2009.

Takaki, Ronald. *A Different Mirror: A History of Multicultural America*. Boston: Little, Brown, 1993.

Tatum, Beverly Daniel. *"Why Are All the Black Kids Sitting Together in the Cafeteria?" And Other Conversations About Race*. New York: Basic Books, 1997.

Taylor, Cheryl A., et al. "The Hillary Clinton Effect: When the Same Role Model Inspires or Fails to Inspire Improved Performance Under Stereotype Threat." *Group Processes and Intergroup Relations* 14 (2011) 447–59.

Thompson, Carl. *Travel Writing*. New York: Routledge, 2011.

Tiberondwa, Ado K. *Missionary Teachers as Agents of Colonialism: A Study of Their Activities in Uganda, 1877–1925*. Kampala, Uganda: Fountain Publishers, 1998.

Tienou, Tite. *The Theological Task of the Church in Africa*. Achimota, Ghana: Africa Christian Press, 1990.

Tillich, Paul. *Theologian of the Boundaries*. Edited by Mark Kline Taylor. Minneapolis: Fortress, 1991.

Trites, Roberta S. *Literary Conceptualizations of Growth: Metaphors and Cognition in Adolescent Literature*. Amsterdam: John Benjamins, 2014.

Tvedt, Terje. "Hydrology and Empire: The Nile, Water Imperialism and the Partition of Africa." *Journal of Imperial and Commonwealth History* 39 (2011) 173–94.

Twiss, Richard. *One Church, Many Tribes: Following Jesus the Way God Made You*. Ventura, CA: Regal, 2000.

Walls, Andrew F. *The Cross-Cultural Process in Christian History: Studies in the Transmission and Appropriation of Faith*. Maryknoll, NY: Orbis, 2002.

———. *The Missionary Movement in Christian History: Studies in the Transmission of Faith*. Maryknoll, NY: Orbis, 1996.

Walls, Andrew F., and Cathy Ross, eds. *Mission in the Twenty-First Century: Exploring the Five Marks of Global Mission*. Maryknoll, NY: Orbis, 2008.

Walton, Gregory M., and Geoffrey L. Cohen. "Stereotype Lift." *Journal of Experimental Social Psychology* 39 (2003) 456–67.

Weinstein, Jeremy M. *Inside Rebellion: The Politics of Insurgent Violence*. New York: Cambridge University Press, 2007.

Weir, Kirsten. "The Pain of Social Rejection." *Monitor on Psychology* 43 (2012) 50–53.

West, Cornel. *Race Matters*. Boston: Beacon, 1993.

Wilson, Francis, and Mamphela Ramphele. *Uprooting Poverty in South Africa*. New York: Hunger Project, 1989.

Winkler, Ingo. *Contemporary Leadership Theories Enhancing the Understanding of the Complexity, Subjectivity and Dynamic of Leadership.* Berlin: Physica-Verlag, 2010.

Winter, Ralph D., and Steven C. Hawthorne, eds. *Perspectives on the World Christian Movement.* Pasadena, CA: William Carey Library, 2009.

Wise, Tim J. *White Like Me.* Brooklyn: Soft Skull, 2005.

Woodberry, J. Dudley, Charles van Engen, and Edgar Elliston, eds. *Missiological Education for the Twenty-First Century: The Book, the Circle, and the Sandals: Essays in Honor of Paul E. Pierson.* American Society of Missiology Series 23. Maryknoll, NY: Orbis, 1996.

Woodberry, Robert. "The Missionary Roots of Liberal Democracy." *American Political Science Review* 106 (2012) 244–74. http://www.hillcountryinstitute.org/wp-content/uploads/missionaryrootsofliberaldemocracy.pdf.

Woodley, Randy S. *Living in Color: Embracing God's Passion for Ethnic Diversity.* Downers Grove, IL: InterVarsity, 2004.

———. "Mission and the Cultural Other: In Search of the Pre-colonial Jesus." *Missiology: An International Review* 43 (2015) 456–68. http://digitalcommons.georgefox.edu/cgi/viewcontent.cgi?article=1049&context=gfes.

"The World's Top Missionary-Sending Country Will Surprise You." *Christianity Today,* July 2013. http://www.christianitytoday.com/pastors/2013/july-online-only/worlds-top-missionary-sending-country-will-surprise-you.html.

Wright, Christopher J. H. *The Mission of God's People: A Biblical Theology of the Church's Mission.* Grand Rapids: Zondervan, 2010.

Zacharias, Ravi. *Walking from East to West: God in the Shadows.* Grand Rapids, MI: Zondervan, 2006.